CROSSING
THE WATER JAMES

KEN PETERS

CREATIVE MINDS PUBLICATIONS

ISBN 979-8-218-73330-8

Library of Congress Control Number: 2025914699

Published by Creative Minds Publications
www.creativemindspublications.com

Contents

What a story! It's very difficult to doubt or question such an honest self-disclosing life story of crossing the cultural, racial, and class divides, as this one. As white Americans, Ken and Becky's 'Crossing the Water James' - in Richmond, Virginia, the former capital of the Confederacy - is a story of persistent, self-sacrificing faith in God. Why did they do this? What for? "To challenge my own racial blindness… by crossing the divides", Ken explains. To reach out and reconcile with African Americans, not doing things to them, but with them, by moving into 'the hood' and living and raising their children among them, serving from the bottom up.

I was really touched, inspired, and challenged by reading their story. I noted Ken specifically says it began when he gave his life to Jesus in 1987: "I began to experience a love in my heart that was undeniable." That led, over time, to a journey of suffering love, not in the name of heroism or political activism, but in the name of Jesus. "While there is a wide chasm between the white and black races in America, there is a bridge. It's the love in God's heart for all humanity, a love that can narrow this great divide."

The more I read their journey, in all that they experienced, the more I saw the picture of Jesus coming on bended knee, stripped of privilege and power, with a basin of water to wash feet, enfolding us into God's reconciling Kingdom of Love.

Ken and Becky's story is greatly needed in our polarized pain-filled societies, for God's sake, for people's sake. I highly recommend this book.

Alexander F Venter, South African Vineyard pastor,
theologian, author, leadership consultant

Ken Peters' work is a powerful example of Christ's love in action. Through the reading club he founded in the inner city, he provides a refuge where children who have experienced trauma find safety, encouragement, and the joy of learning. He and Becky's faithful commitment to serving the underserved reflect God's heart for the vulnerable.

Richard Verlander, author/speaker
Rocks Across the Pond, The Shelter Gang and Their Secret Adventure

"Small things done with great love will change the world." Ironically, it is what may seem minuscule in the eyes of the world that becomes a profound tool in God's toolkit.

Do you want to change your part of this broken world? Step one is catching a God-breathed, doable vision that has God's fingerprints on it. There's a story in you waiting to get out. Soak in Ken's story and yours will become clear.

Steve Sjogren
Author, *Conspiracy of Kindness*

To Becky,

You are the love of my life. Your ability to see beauty in often overlooked places and people continually brings me joy and inspiration- and stretches me. Thank you for walking with God so faithfully through the years-and with me.

Foreword

Crossing the Water James is a must read for anyone desiring to be a part of the racial healing we all need. It is the authentic journey of Ken and Becky Peters choosing to be vulnerable and immersing themselves (with humility) into the craziness of the racial dysfunction of Richmond, Virginia (the former Capital of the Confederacy). Naively, yet with the Godly intentions of making a real difference, this is their story of intentionally moving into the city. With hearts of perseverance, they press through the long story of building relationships through all the twists and turns of real life. *Crossing the Water James* offers learning and healing that will benefit all who read it.

As a lifelong resident of Richmond, *Crossing the Water James* hits home because I believe racial healing is key to the future flourishing of the "new Richmond" aka RVA. This book is so full of the beautiful application of how one lives their faith quietly in public view without being religious. It is simply being available to be used by God to press back injustice through love in action. Thus, their example of lived faith and love can be applied anywhere.

Yet, Ken and Becky discovered the harsh realities of broken systems and their unjust impacts on the urban poor. They learn to adjust by choosing to stay in real enduring relationships while also staying in the posture of students. As learners they accept and teach others that broad brushed stereotypes only continue to fuel the brokenness. Their perseverance evolves into true empathy and love that comes to life due to their proximity to the real lived experiences of everyday people in their neighborhood. Ken and Becky show us how to grow in loving the way Jesus wants all of us to intentionally love our neighbors.

Read this book then go and live what you learn from it; your life and the lives of others will be better if you do!

Donald L. Coleman
Co-Founding Pastor of East End Fellowship
(Former Chairman) Richmond Public Schools
Board of Trustees, 2015

CROSSING THE WATER JAMES

Introduction

"That's across the water, Mr. Peters!"

This strange response came from a twelve-year-old African-American girl attending a weekly reading club that we had recently started in our home for neighborhood children. While I can't recall the exact context of our conversation, her emphatic and odd reply caught me off guard. I begin thinking to myself. *What water? What is she talking about?*

After a bit more conversation, I realized she was referring to the James River. This sizable river flows west to east through the heart of our city, creating the Northside and Southside of Richmond, Virginia. While Richmond was officially founded in 1737 by William Byrd II, the territory was first claimed on behalf of England on May 24, 1607, by explorers Christopher Newport and John Smith. They had come up the river from Jamestown, Virginia, until their navigation was terminated by the rapids on the fall line, where Richmond now sits. It was here that Newport planted a cross, claiming the land for King James I of England, and thus naming the river after the king.

Having spent most of my life in the Richmond area, I knew the river had sometimes been an impediment for travelers, due to the tolls that were charged to cross several bridges. More than that, however, it has proved to be a psychological barrier over the years. People say things such as, "I don't cross the river." There are those from the Northside who don't care much for the Southside of the river and vice versa. I'm not sure where this geographical prejudice originated, but regardless, this was the first time I had heard the James River referred to as, *the water*. I would later hear it called this by numerous other African-American children.

This twelve-year old's innocent response about a body of water was one of many educational moments I would experience as I stepped into a culture that I thought I knew something about. Her simple statement would prove to be a metaphor for an even deeper and wider chasm than I ever knew existed-the black and white racial divide.

A few years prior, my wife and I had moved our family from a northern suburb of Richmond into a predominantly African-American neighborhood in South Richmond with the idea of bringing racial reconciliation to our city. Now this may sound a bit idealistic or perhaps even foolish. Why would we ever disrupt our relatively stable family life to pursue something so seemingly impossible? We were moved by our faith and a sense that God had called us to cross the water. As we stepped out in response to this call, we had no idea of all that God had in mind for us along the way. While we had a somewhat utopian vision of racial unity, it would be on this journey that much of the preconceived and misperceptions I had of the African American race would be exposed, along with my residual racial prejudice.

When did I first become consciously aware of prejudicial thoughts within myself? It was in 1987 when I became serious about my faith. I knelt beside my bed one day and surrendered my life to Jesus. While this was truly a pivotal moment in my life, there were no lights from heaven or angels singing, that I was aware of anyway. Yet, from that moment on, things were noticeably different. I began to experience a love in my heart that was undeniable. I started to realize that much of the narrative of race that I had learned in the first thirty years of my life was contrary to the heart of God. I began to see the world and other people in a different light. I felt a love for others that was deeper and more genuine than anything I had ever experienced before.

This led me to ask some questions. *Why did I still have certain thoughts pass through my mind that I was ashamed of?* I didn't want them and yet, occasionally they would still pop up. *Why am I this way? How did I become a man who still has prejudicial thoughts?*

In this book, I want to offer a way across this great racial divide-a bridge if you will. It's the way of the heart. In particular, the way of God's heart. Honestly, while there are occasional glimpses of God's heart as it relates to racial justice, it's still a pretty rare occurrence. There are some advances and reforms that have occurred; however, it is a slow and arduous labor that can be frustrating. Like gravity, there seems to be tangible resistance. It often appears hopeless. Is it?

Somewhere in the midst of this is God's heart. The bible tells us that God is love. The bible also tells us that there will come a day when people from every tribe, nation, language and people will gather before him and he will wipe away every tear. It's what we refer to as heaven. But what about now? It's this same love that led God to take on human flesh in the person of Jesus to show us what this love looks like and how we can walk in it-this side of heaven. Jesus, when demonstrating this way of life, effectively brought heaven to earth. This means that the unity of humanity is available now, as we allow God's heart to become our own.

Dr. Martin Luther King, Jr. described this when he said, "But the end is reconciliation; the end is redemption; the end is the creation of the beloved community. It is this type of spirit and this type of love that can transform opposers into friends. It is this type of understanding goodwill that will transform the deep gloom of the old age into the exuberant gladness of the new age. It is this love which will bring about miracles in the hearts of men."

Is this an idealistic fantasy that has nothing to do with living in the real world? Is it just wishful thinking or some unattainable dream? Who wouldn't want to live in a world like this? Well, truth be told, there are hate-filled voices who oppose this, but we must not let them seize the conversation. Dr. King was inspired by the Christian scriptures and a faith in which Jesus described just such a world-a humanity that lives out of God's desire for us to walk in unity, with a love for one another.

It was Jesus who said, "Repent, for the Kingdom of Heaven is at hand." This word repent comes from the Greek word, *metanoia* which means to change our way of thinking. Where we begin to see every human being, regardless of race or ethnicity, as being made in the image of God, the *Imago Dai*.

In other words, we have been thinking that life is one way, when in fact there is another way-a more desirable way, a way that leads to a peaceable and equitable humanity. What if we were to give it a try? What if we intentionally asked God to align our hearts with His? Can you imagine the ripple effects that might follow this way of love?

This book follows my family's personal journey across a bridge, a literal bridge across the James River, but also a bridge across the racial divide. It is a journey through my own naivety, where I would have many assumptions challenged and my heart exposed. I would also feel my heart expand with a love for people of a different race, especially their children growing up in very challenging circumstances.

While there is a wide chasm between the white and black races in America, there is a bridge. It's the love in God's heart for all humanity, and a love that can narrow this great divide. If there is any hope for healing the racial strife in our country, I believe it must begin with honesty, total honesty with ourselves and a willingness to admit that we might be wrong about some things. This can allow us to truly see others, regardless of our initial impressions, but this time though, we are looking through God's eyes and heart. I believe an honest evaluation of ourselves is the first step towards healing the racial divide. If we're willing to do that, then God is faithful to shine the light on the path forward, our next steps.

In the following chapters you will journey with my family across the bridge into a new community. You'll witness my prejudice, my naivety, and my heart exposed. My hope is that I represent God well in telling it and that others may hear a call to join me on this quest. Your journey will be your journey, but my prayer is that it will cross the same bridge as mine, the bridge of love.

This story is not one of continual victories and success, although I have witnessed some incredible moments. It is a story about challenging my own racial blindness. I invite you to walk with me in this story and see what God may impart to your heart that will help us together see the racial divide narrow in our lifetime. Join me as we move toward the day when this divide will ultimately cease to exist.

Chapter One

The Formative Years

The first twelve years of my life were idyllic in many ways. I lived in the same house and attended the same church and for most of my childhood went to the same school. My best friend, Mark, also lived next door the entire time. Some of my earliest memories were typical of a white, middle-class boy growing up in the 1960s. Dad worked a 9-5 job at a local industrial plant. Mom kept house, kept children and kept up with the afternoon soap operas on TV. When I wasn't in school or doing my homework, you could find me in front of the TV watching the latest adventures of Superman or perhaps laughing at Barney (not the big, purple dinosaur). Sheriff Andy Taylor's sidekick on the Andy Griffith Show was the Barney of the sixties.

If my older brothers got to the television first, I'd often be out cruising the streets on my bike. I loved the adventure of exploring the furthermost reaches of the neighborhood. I was always on the lookout for discarded glass soda bottles to exchange for cash at the local store. Mostly, I just enjoyed the freedom of being on my own and wherever the streets might take me (except for the one house with a very overzealous, protective dog). He seemed to own the yard and sometimes the street. There was also the spooky house where one of my friends lived. Supposedly, it was used as a hospital during the Civil War. My friend told me there were tunnels underneath that were used to take dead soldiers out back to a field for burial. Maybe that was true. Maybe it was a wine cellar. Who knows? I wasn't interested in going down there.

If it was a weekday, regardless of what adventure I might be on, I had to make sure I was home by 6pm for dinner. I was expected to be on time, have my hands washed and eat whatever was placed before me because mom didn't hesitate to remind me that there were "starving children in Africa."

Most Saturdays, Mark and I would receive small allowances from our dads, and we would go to the Community Mart at the end of our street. The store was on the opposite side of his house from us and was one of our favorite hangouts. In those days, you could buy a piece of gum or candy for a penny. With the change jingling and burning a hole in our pockets, we would hurry down to the store. Sometimes we'd get there before it opened and knock loudly on the door. The storeowners lived above the store and were usually good-natured about the early morning wake-up calls.

We lived just three blocks from the Virginia State Fairgrounds. I loved watching the nightly fireworks from our house when the fair was in town each fall. Me, mom and my siblings would take turns claiming each successive display to see who would end up with the grand finale. I don't recall winning a prize for that creative little game, but we sure had a lot of fun. The fairgrounds were also the home to NASCAR racing in the spring and fall. I loved hearing the roar of the engines making their way into our neighborhood. They also hosted Friday night professional wrestling matches. One Friday night, when I was around ten years old, I walked by myself to watch the famous African American boxer Joe Lewis referee the matches. After retiring from boxing, he traveled the wrestling circuit for several years. This particular night culminated with him getting into a fake fist fight with one of the wrestlers. As a boxing and wrestling fan, I loved it. Afterwards, I crossed a busy thoroughfare and made my way home through the dark neighborhood streets. Apart from a little apprehension of walking alone in the dark, I generally felt that all was well in my world.

I didn't realize at the time, but my care-free and insulated childhood was about to change dramatically. I was eleven years old when For Sale signs suddenly appeared on every street I would walk or ride down. What was going on?

It was late 1968, when I began to hear rumblings of some cataclysmic event that was apparently descending upon our nice little American dream life. What could possibly be so earth shattering that my world as I knew it was about to be turned upside down? It turns out that a neighbor just a few houses down the street had sold their home to a black family. From the frantic talk that ensued, you would have thought our neighborhood was under attack by an invading foreign army. Suddenly, For Sale signs seemed to pop up overnight. The safe little world in which I was beginning to gain some confidence as a young boy suddenly came crashing down.

Prior to all this happening, I was relatively insulated from the black community. I had no black friends. I attended the all-white Laburnum Elementary School in nearby Henrico County. Even though the U.S. Supreme Court decision of Brown vs. Board of Education had legally integrated the public school system in 1954, it would take years for many school districts to comply. Even as they did, demographics would often still reflect the heart of segregation as people resisted the integration. This was true of my Little League Baseball team as well. We had no black kids participating in 1969. I truly lived in a "white bubble."

Randolph was the only black person I ever encountered on a regular basis. He worked at the Texaco gas station a block away. He didn't seem particularly threatening. Now, why would I say that? You see, all I knew of black people, or negroes as they were politely called in the south, was how they were presented- always in a negative way. I heard things like, "We don't go into that part of town" or "They're not like us." So, it's no wonder that my conclusion as a young boy was that black people must be dangerous. Not surprisingly, I had a vivid dream one night of a gang of marauding black men walking behind my house wearing black berets looking to hurt someone. I woke up trembling in fear. I also heard lies like, "They're lazy" or "They're not as intelligent as we are." I have no childhood recollection of anyone challenging these insidious assertions.

It didn't take long for a For Sale sign to appear in our yard and my friend's yard next door. Little did I know at the time, but our family was participating in what was known as white flight. Merriam-Webster dictionary defines this as, "the departure of whites from places (such as urban neighborhoods or schools) increasingly or predominantly populated by minorities." There are several factors that helped create this phenomenon of white flight, but it was a choice that many white families made to avoid the legal reality of desegregation.

One of those factors was the *1954 Brown v. Board of Education* Supreme Court ruling. Brown included five cases brought against the Board of Education, including one from Prince Edward County Virginia. This landmark decision by the U.S. Supreme Court found that segregation by race in the public school system was unconstitutional. It violated the *equal protection clause* of the

14th amendment. Prior to this, our public education system operated under the *separate but equal* doctrine that had been established in the *1896 Plessy v. Ferguson* ruling by the Supreme Court. In other words, there were black schools and white schools. However, they were anything but equal.

Once the *Brown v. Board* decision became the law of the land, there was great resistance. It would take years in many localities for integration to occur with some degree of success. Virginia pushed back hard. Senator Harry F. Byrd Sr. developed a strategy called Massive Resistance where he would push for laws to resist desegregation. In Prince Edward County, the public schools would be defunded by the County Board of Supervisors, effectively closing all the public schools-black and white. A private school, Prince Edward Academy, was established for the white students. The black students of the county would have no school access from 1959 until 1963. While lawsuits were slowly making their way through the courts, the Kennedy Administration provided funds along with private donors to establish the Black Free Schools in 1963. It wouldn't be until the following year that the Supreme Court ordered Prince Edward Public Schools to reopen.

The damage was done, particularly to the youngest of students. In her book, *Something Must Be Done About Prince Edward County*, Kristen Green describes the effect this had on one young boy who was 10 years old before he started school. "Ricky was poor, and his teachers wrote him off, applying the same low expectations that black children too often face in school today. 'They knew where I was from and knew I'd been left behind," he told me. "'They couldn't hold back a whole class to help me.'"

How could it be that black students were denied an education for five years? How could a community of mostly kind, thoughtful and loving people support such an injustice?

Fear and ignorance were often used to appeal to the white community for support of segregation policies and laws. And they would say that they were looking out for their children's welfare, doing what was best for their family. They believed that educational standards would be lowered if black and white children were in the same classes. There was fear of white teen girls getting pregnant by black males. And there was fear of interracial marriages, which was illegal in Virginia until 1967 when another landmark Supreme Court case, *Loving v. Virginia*, would repeal this law. Even though the legal battles to resist integration would ultimately fail, practical resistance would continue for years to come, even to this very day.

I believe the fears that had been planted in the minds and hearts of the white community, helped fuel this white flight that I suddenly found myself swept up in. This continual resistance to integration would have destructive effects on both the black and white communities going forward, including me and my friend, Mark.

One day, during the spring of 1969, Mark and I sat talking in his front yard. We didn't understand why we had to move. We weren't aware of all the legal maneuverings that had been occurring throughout our lives. We just heard that black people were taking over our neighborhood and it was no longer safe to live here. Well, that's what we surmised from overhearing the conversations. We didn't want to move. We were best friends. We had shared so much of life together. While he was a year younger, he always lived next door to me. On weekends we would often hang out at each other's houses, watching TV or playing with our GI Joes. We played baseball in the backyard with his dad who was also a huge University of Virginia football fan. He would take us to home games in Charlottesville. He even took us to an away game at Virginia Tech one year which was about a four-hour drive from Richmond. And of course, we cruised the neighborhood streets together, mostly staying out of trouble.

Both of our houses sold quickly, and just before my twelfth birthday, we moved. Mark's family ended up in a suburban neighborhood in Henrico County on the west side of Richmond. Our family headed to the newly emerging suburbs of Hanover County on the north side of the city. We would both be joining other white families who had made similar moves from the shifting demographics of Richmond. Our parents, sensitive to our plight and loss, managed

Here I am ready to take on the world

to arrange a few get-togethers after we moved. But, as time moved on and we established new social networks, these post-exile visits gradually ended.

Where did I land at the tender, impressionable age of twelve? Even though it was only seven miles from our Richmond home, it seemed as though we had moved across the country. The contrast from city life to this new suburban countryside was stark. Hanover County is not just any rural area of the country. This is the land where several battles were fought during the Civil War, The War between the States, The War of Northern Aggression, Mr. Lincoln's War, or The War of the Rebellion-the name differs depending on who you ask or where you were raised. Either way, I found myself surrounded by many defensive earthworks designed to protect the Confederate army and subsequently Richmond from the Yankees. It wasn't surprising that many of the local institutions were named in honor of Southern heroes or events. For example, we moved into a neighborhood called Brandy Creek rumored to have been named after a creek that flowed red with blood during some of the fierce fighting that took place nearby.

In the fall of 1969, I entered the seventh grade at Battlefield Park Elementary. This was a K-7 school. Our yearbook was called The Rebel. Had we not moved, I would have attended Henrico High School, which had grades 7-12 at the time. Attending an elementary school in 7th grade felt like a demotion to me. Prior to us moving, my sixth-grade teacher polled our class to find out what school we would attend the following year. Most of my classmates said they were going to Henrico High School. When my turn came and I sheepishly told them I would be attending Battlefield Park Elementary School, quiet laughter ensued. That was the least of the challenges that I would soon be facing.

One of the first memories I had of my new school was walking into a classroom and seeing two boys standing by an open window in the back. I wondered what they were staring at outside the window. The teacher hadn't arrived yet, so I made my way toward them to see what was so interesting. As I got closer, I saw that they were chewing tobacco and spitting out the window of our second-floor classroom. What in the world? Where was I? Like Dorothy said in The Wizard of Oz, "Toto, I've a feeling we're not in Kansas anymore." Those two guys would eventually become my friends.

It was at Battlefield Park that I first went to school with black students. How ironic-isn't that why we moved? However, I was told that black people in Hanover were different. Apparently, the black kids I was now going to school with were "country blacks" (to put it kindly), nothing like the "city blacks". Early on I became aware that one of the black girls in my class had a crush on me. This was quite confusing for a young boy who was just awakening to the opposite sex while also having my first up-close exposure to a different race of people. While there was something attractive about the attention, I resisted her overtures. I don't know if it was because of my generational prejudice or my inexperience with girls. I'm sure it was a combination of both. Little did I know at the time, but there was a fourth-grade student there who would eventually become my wife.

Moving on from elementary school, I attended Stonewall Jackson Junior High for 8th and 9th grade. Again, our yearbook was The Rebel. From 10th through 12th grade, I attended Lee-Davis High School. It was named after the famous Confederate Civil War general, Robert E. Lee and the President of the Confederacy, Jefferson Davis. Our yearbook was The Confederate. During our home football games, one of our school mascots would ride his horse across the field waving a Confederate flag. By this time, I was becoming acclimated to the culture, and this was just a typical Friday night for me-hanging with my friends and cheering on our Confederates.

This wouldn't be the case for everyone. A few years back, I met a black man who used to play for one of the Richmond City football teams back in the 70's. He told me how they used to be afraid to come out to Hanover County to play us. He said that people would yell expletives at them as they would be pulling away on the bus after the game. I don't remember participating or witnessing that behavior, but I don't doubt his experience. It certainly left a haunting impression on this man.

As the fumes of social consciousness and the drug-induced enlightenment of the 1960's made their way into the 1970's and into my social network, we now had a "cool" black friend hanging out with us. In some strange way, the drug culture seemed to be a bridge between the races as we did sometimes party together. I believe we were self-medicating from the harsh realities we were growing up in, including this strange racial divide. Sometimes, me and my "cool" friend would drag-race one another in our vehicles. I drove my powerful Mustang II, and he drove his equally impressive VW Bug. We tied every race. Thinking back, this was probably the only truly equal footing we stood on at the time. In hindsight,

I think the challenging thing for me and most of my white friends was the stark contrast of the generational prejudice we were raised in and the idealism of youth. The racial stuff seemed to take a back seat to the typical teen-age stuff we'd do together.

Even as me and my friends took some steps across this bridge of reconciliation, the deep-seated generational prejudice in the community was not ready to join us. One night my friends and I stopped by my house to hang out for a while. By this time, I was accustomed to having my black friend around. We came in through the front door and went down to the basement to watch TV. When I went back upstairs to get us something to drink, I was confronted by one of my parents with the unexpected question, "What is HE doing here?"

It never crossed my mind that his presence in our home might be an issue. I went downstairs and stalled for a few minutes, trying to act normally. I then made some flimsy excuses that we had to leave. I'm sure the real reason wasn't lost on my friend. He didn't deserve that treatment from me or my family. It brings tears to my eyes as I write this today. I begin to try and imagine the many rejections he must have felt time and time again in his formative years and how this must have shaped his life. I think of the relationships he never had the opportunity to experience because of racial prejudice.

It was because of this same prejudice that I lost my relationship with my childhood friend. I wouldn't see Mark again until we happened upon one another in a softball game fifteen years after we moved. It was quite a surprise to see him after all these years. We spoke briefly before the game and said how great it was to see each other again. Then it was game time.

The score stayed close throughout the game. It was the bottom of the seventh inning (the last inning) with two outs and a runner on second base. Our team was down by one run. Mark was playing in the outfield and as it turned out, it was my turn to bat. I was very confident in my ability to drop a ball in play and advance the runner. However, the old rivalry and competitive spirit rose in me. I wanted a walk-off home run or at least an extra-base hit to show off to my old friend. I got a good pitch and hit it hard. I took off for first base knowing I had at least tied the game. It felt good! I rounded the bag and watched in disbelief as another outfielder, on a dead run, reached low and snagged the fading ball. And just like that, the thrill of victory was snagged by the agony of defeat.

After the game, Mark and I laughed about it and talked briefly about getting together and catching up. I would see my friend only one more time. It was a few years later after I read an obituary in the newspaper of his father's passing. I visited the funeral home where once again we would talk about getting together, but we never did. Mark was my good childhood friend, but as it turned out, our friendship was just another casualty of racial prejudice and the distance it created.

This is just a glimpse into my childhood and some of the prejudices I was introduced to over time. These were very formative years where previous generations (parents and grandparents) passed down their prejudicial values to the next generation (me and my siblings). I didn't realize it at the time, but I was becoming generationally prejudiced. I don't believe anyone can be raised in an environment like I was and not have ingrained thought patterns and emotional responses. I believe this is what happened to my parents, their parents, and their parents before them. I am generationally prejudiced, but I am prejudiced, nonetheless. To this day, when I encounter a person of color, it's still possible to have a negative thought cross my mind simply because of the prejudicial input I received during my formative years. Fortunately, I have come to a place where I tend to recognize them and can dismiss them.

Another name for this is implicit bias. This term was first coined in 1995 by psychologists Mahazrin Banaji and Anthony Greenwald. This is where we make assessments in our subconscious, without intentionally or consciously thinking about a person or situation. We're usually not even aware that we are thinking or acting in a certain way. For example, in some social settings, a white person may gravitate towards a seat with other white people rather than joining a group of black people in the same room. This isn't always an intentional act; it's a subconscious decision.

Implicit bias is different from willfully embracing prejudice or racism. While that is still very much a reality today, I'm not addressing this specifically. I'm speaking to how our biases or prejudices are formed to begin with. Once we become aware of their existence within us, we can begin to recognize the influence they have on us and others. We can then reject the biases that are harmful and choose actions that are helpful or considerate. Awareness is the first step.

Now, I am acutely aware of how the word prejudice has been used to the point where its meaning can be lost. Even worse, where its fruit is never truly examined. What does it mean to be prejudiced? In its most basic form, it means to pre-judge something. We can be prejudiced about any number of things. For example, I don't like deviled eggs. I don't like the smell of deviled eggs. I don't like to watch people eat deviled eggs. I refuse to eat deviled eggs no matter how many times my wife Becky offers them to me and tells me how delicious they are. There is one important factor to understand, though. I've never eaten a deviled egg. Yet, I have pre-judged them all. I am prejudiced when it comes to deviled eggs.

All kidding aside, the unfortunate truth is that we also pre-judge people or situations. We are born into a world filled with this reality. Does that mean we are all born prejudiced? I'll leave that question to the theologians and philosophers. Either way, whether we are born with a clean slate or a tarnished one, we are quickly thrust into an imperfect world-one filled with prejudice and its natural outcome, systemic racism.

Why would I be suspicious of a black person I meet for the first time if I had not in some way been shaped and formed to have some bias that I believe to be true of an entire race? It happened both subtly and systemically through my childhood environment. Although after reading my story, you may say there was nothing subtle about it. The point is that the prejudice that resides in me resulted from a day-to-day immersion that found its way into my subconscious more so than through formal education.

However, it would be an injustice to ignore the systemic forces that reinforced the generational prejudice I received. A system of segregation effectively kept me separated from black America for the first twelve years of my life. The exceptions being those rare excursions through visiting "that part of town" and the few black characters on TV. Robert Lichter in "Prime-time Prejudice: TV's Images of Black and Hispanics", says "that according to research on the portrayal of African American in prime-time television from 1955-1986, only 6 percent of the characters were African American."

My formal education of the black experience in America was also sparse and often sanitized. For example, my seventh grade Virginia history book, entitled Virginia: History- Government-Geography reads, "life among the Negroes of Virginia in slavery times was generally happy. The Negroes went about in a cheerful manner making a living for themselves and for those for whom they worked."

All of this is in the past, right? Things are different now. We've come a long way in race relations since the 1970's. Allow me to push back on that just a bit. I currently work with at-risk children in the city of Richmond. One day, I was picking up a few kids to take them to a local camp for a few days. They live in one of Richmond's Public Housing Projects. As I stood on the front porch talking with Mom, a man stepped out of the apartment next door. He appeared to be in his early thirties. He overheard our conversation and asked me where the camp was located. I told him it was Camp Hanover.

He replied, "They don't like our kind out there." I was taken aback. I can't remember what I said to him. I recall fumbling around for something kind to say, all the while wondering to myself, can this still be true?

As if this question was spoken aloud and heard by God himself, its reality was brought home just a few days later. I was sitting on the front porch texting our Godson Devin, who now lives near Seattle, Washington. He was born and raised in South Richmond and would become family to us. I'll share more of his story a little later. After living and raising our family in South Richmond for twenty-four years, Becky and I recently moved back to Hanover. Devin hasn't been home for several years and hasn't seen our new place. Even though he hasn't been out here yet, he refers to it as "the boondocks." I told him we would love for him to visit whenever he gets back to Richmond.

Replying to my invitation, he texted.

Devin: I don't know if my people are welcomed, unless a lot of stuff has changed in the world since I left.

Ken: You are our people, and we are trying to be a bridge out here in Hanover.

Devin: When it's built let me know, lol. I won't have to think twice about coming out there, lol.

This was 2024. Can this still be true? If so, is bridging the racial divide even possible? Do the races even desire to come together? We can become so overwhelmed with the enormity of the issues related to race that we sometimes want to throw up our hands and say, "It's hopeless. Things will never change. It's always been this way."

We can suffer from racial fatigue when we're just tired of hearing and talking about it. Perhaps we wonder, "What could I ever do?" Now, I believe that's a great question, one worth repeating and one worth pondering.

There's a scripture in the bible that says, "Perfect love casts out fear." I believe that prejudice is rooted in fear-mostly, the fear of the unknown. In our fear we are tempted to put up walls of defense. We try to protect ourselves. I believe there's another way. Instead of living behind a wall of fear and suspicion, what if we take a step onto a bridge, a bridge that already exists-a bridge of love?

Our role is to take an intentional step towards those that are different from us. As we do, something happens in our hearts that we cannot produce on our own. With each tentative and vulnerable step, we take across the bridge. We begin to experience love taking root in our hearts. I believe this love is already present and available. It's simply waiting for us to step into it. And as we experience more of this love, we are moved to take the next step across the bridge, and the next. As our hearts begin to experience a deepening love, our actions begin to line up with our hearts. Does love produce action, or does action produce love? Well, I think it's both. It's in this process that the chasm between the races begins to narrow, certainly between our heart and the one we move toward.

When I first took a step on this bridge, I was full of naivety. Yet, with each step I took, I was met with a comforting love that seemed to remind me that I was on the right path. I found a growing love for those who were different from me. Something had changed in me-it felt right. It felt good. It felt hopeful. Now, I am aware that this word love can be a bit nebulous. What does it really mean? In the pages that follow, I hope the answer to that question will emerge with increasing clarity in your heart as we walk across this bridge together. Reconciliation is not only desirable; it really is possible.

While everyone's journey across this bridge will look different, mine included my wife, Becky, and me leaving our suburban home and moving into a predominantly black neighborhood in Richmond's Southside. It was here that we would raise our children in a different environment than we had experienced growing up. We were about to embark on an education that we thought we knew something about but soon came to discover just how little we really knew.

Chapter 2

Can You Spell Naivety?

So, how did we arrive at the decision to move our family into a black neighborhood in the first place? The decision came pretty easily, however, getting there would take some perseverance. The year was 1996. Twenty-seven years had passed since my childhood had suddenly been interrupted by that fateful move to Hanover County. Becky and I had been married for twelve years and were raising a growing family. We had been back in Hanover for six years after spending a year at Asbury Seminary in Wilmore, Kentucky preparing for the ministry. During that time, we connected with the Association of Vineyard Churches and were in the early stages of launching a new Vineyard church in Richmond. Life was exciting and very full.

It was around this same time that Becky attended a seminar on racial reconciliation at a downtown church. The speakers included Wellington Boone, a local black pastor, and John Dawson, a white minister and author of the book, *Healing America's Wounds*. They shared a compelling message of reconciliation for the black and white communities. Pastor Boone encouraged white families to move into black neighborhoods with a vision of unity in mind. Now, gentrification is another unfortunate part of this story-unintentional, yes, but a reality, nonetheless.

As Becky listened to the message, she sensed God's heart for reconciliation and was moved to tears. She was beginning to see with clarity the great racial divide that still exists today. She came home excited to share the details with me. As we sat and talked about it, my heart was moved as well. And we began to wonder, *is this something we should consider?* As the days passed, we began to think seriously about moving into the city. Our hearts were already engaged, and now our minds were becoming consumed with the possibility. As we began to share our idea with friends and family, we received a fair amount of push-back. "You'd better be sure you are called to go there! It could be dangerous! People get killed in the city!" To which we responded, "We think we are. We hope we are. How can we know for sure?"

Remember, this was the mid-1990's. Our nation was just emerging from the recent crack cocaine epidemic and the violence that decimated many urban families. A local Richmond reporter put it this way, *"The city was all-but killed by the skyrocketing murder rates during the crack cocaine years in the late 1980s through the mid-90s. It peaked in 1994 with 161 slayings, making Richmond the second deadliest city - per capita - in the nation."*

This was long before gentrification would take hold and compound the devastating effects on black families. Gentrification is when people with higher incomes move into a community of lower-income residents, who are often labeled people of color. This brings an increase in property values and rents which often results in the displacement of the current residents.

Our friends' and family's concerns were understandable and not unwarranted. Who would exchange an established and secure suburban life for all the challenges the city offered, especially in a low-economic black community? I guess we would. So, we decided to go for it.

The first thing we had to do was put our house on the market to sell. Becky is a realtor, so she got the process moving. We had a 4 bedroom, 2 ½ bath home that sat on a huge lot and was in a great school district. Since it was sure to sell right away, we needed to find a home in the city as soon as possible. We quickly came across one we loved. It was in one of the historical neighborhoods in Richmond called Woodland Heights. It was near the divide between a white neighborhood and a black neighborhood. It was "just across the tracks." This phrase has been used over the years to describe the dividing line between poor and more wealthy residents of a community, sometimes by literal railroad tracks. For us, the tracks were in fact a busy street, Forest Hill Avenue.

In our excitement, we told our family and friends about the house and began preparing for the move. There was just one problem. Our contract contained a *first right of refusal clause*. This means that if a non-contingent contract was placed on the house by another purchaser before we sold our current home, we would have 48 hours for it to sell or come up with the money another way. Unfortunately, our lovely suburban home had yet to receive an offer and someone else did come along and purchase our dream home in the city.

As you can imagine, we were disappointed, but we were also determined to keep looking. It wouldn't take long for us to get our hopes up again. This time it came from an unusual source. One day, Becky happened to notice the tag on a washcloth in our bathroom. It listed the manufacturer's name, *By Dundee*. Becky remembered a street named Dundee in the area where we had been looking. She searched the current home listings to see if by chance a house was for sale on that particular street. And sure enough, just across Forest Hill Avenue and into the black community, there was a house for sale on Dundee Ave. Perseverance was finally paying off and this time we had a sign that this was divine providence. Now, that's the kind of guidance I need. It was almost written in the sky.

We took the children and toured the house. It did need some TLC, and we would have to get creative with the sleeping areas, but it would work for us. We put a contract on the new house, also with a *first right of refusal clause*. Full of faith, we were excited that this was finally coming to pass. We had lowered the price on our Hanover home, and we were certain that this would get it sold. And so, when the listing agent called Becky to tell her that someone else had put a contract on the Dundee house, full of faith she responded, "That's Ok. Our house is going to sell." Those 48 hours came and went with no sale of our home. Someone else had purchased the home that we were sure was to be ours.

The disappointment was profound. Maybe this was a crazy idea after all. *Were we just some disillusioned idealists?* We were also embarrassed having shared with others how God was leading us. I can only imagine some of the thoughts our friends and family must have had about our decision-making skills.

In my attempt to comfort and reassure Becky, I said to her, "Well, the tag didn't say Buy Dundee. It said, By Dundee." Maybe that means our house will be near Dundee."

It turned out that there was a house for sale on an adjacent street a couple of blocks from Dundee. We decided to look at it. We loved it; it was full of charm

15

and character. It had a beautiful big backyard for the children to play in. We decided to head home so that Becky could write an offer on it. We left the house and came upon an intersection. Just as I began to turn left, Becky looked across the street and saw a brick Cape Cod. The trim paint was weathered and peeling, the screen was ripped out of the side porch, a gutter was hanging down to the ground, and there was trash scattered throughout the yard. And there was a little sign in the window that said *NOTICE*.

We pulled up in front and parked. We got out and walked over to the house to read the sign. It turns out that it was a foreclosure and up for auction. Becky said, "If it has a finished basement, it's ours." We knelt and peeked through a basement window and saw wood paneled walls. It was a beautiful home. Well, let's just say we had vision for it. Oh, and the street it was on? Dundee!

The very next day, Becky received a call from a real estate agent inquiring about our house for sale. During the conversation, Becky mentioned that we found a foreclosure to purchase. While our house wasn't going to work for this agent's client, she had a lot of experience with foreclosures and was willing to help us through the process. The next thing you know, we're sitting in a small room at city hall in downtown Richmond where the sealed bid envelopes were opened and announced to the gathered crowd. There were three bids for this particular house. The first was a little under the asking price. The second one was the exact asking price. We breathed a sigh of relief, knowing our bid was a little higher. When ours was read aloud, there was a palpable silence in the room. It was as if the experienced bidders were saying to themselves, who are these people-a naive white family about to begin a journey into Black America-that's who.

One problem remained. We still hadn't received a contract for our current home. Here we go again. We had already lowered the price a couple of times and still had no interest. We thought about renting it. That is if we could get a mortgage on the city house along with our current one. However, qualifying for two mortgage payments was a long shot.

Within a week of us winning the bid on the Dundee house, a stranger showed up at our home one day. Becky opened the door and stepped onto the front porch. She pulled the door shut behind her, not wanting this man to see our well-lived-in home. By this time, we had given up trying to keep it presentable for prospective buyers. He began to explain that his ex-wife had looked at our house a few months prior and thought he might be interested in it. Becky said to him, "Come on in. Don't mind the mess." After only looking around the first floor, on the way down the basement steps, he said, "I'll take it!" And, he didn't have a realtor. So, he used Becky as his agent, saving us a considerable amount of money. And just like that, our decision to move into the city was now becoming a reality.

We closed on our city home in November of 1997. In addition to packing up our current place, we had three weeks to clean and repair a home that, according to the neighbors, had recently been used as a drug house. I wasn't sure what they meant by that, and I didn't ask. Evidently, the elderly woman who had lived there for years had died and her surviving family had not kept up with the payments, so it had gone into foreclosure.

It was obvious that the upkeep on the house had been neglected for some time. There was a lot of work to be done. The very first thing we had to do was set off pesticide smoke bombs to clear the house of a bug infestation. This was followed by thorough scrubbing from top to bottom. The upstairs bedrooms had five layers of wallpaper covering the original plaster walls. I spent days scraping the paper off. In one bedroom, the bottom layer was a 1950's era western theme. This was followed by putting a lot of paint on the walls. Thankfully, we had some great friends from church who pitched in to help us. They were truly a Godsend.

As we worked feverishly preparing the home for our arrival, we were amazed at the quality we found. The dining room chandelier was beautiful with its glass prisms reflecting the light. The living room was accented by plaster crown molding and hardwood floors. While the custom 1950 metal kitchen cabinets took a while to grow on us, we came to love them. The house was situated so that the kitchen windows faced east welcoming the morning sun. It also had a laundry chute from the upstairs to the basement. Later we would hear from one of our adult children how they had explored and traveled this chute as a child. It sat on 2 ½ city lots with plenty of room for the children to play outside. It was obvious to us that the original owners had put a lot of thought and money into building this home.

One day while we were moving our stuff into the house, one of our new neighbors came over to meet us. He said, "You know who built this house, don't you? Joe Ukrop." We didn't know that. Mr. Ukrop was a well-known local grocer who started a successful family grocery chain in the Richmond area. He opened his first store in 1937 on Hull Street in South Richmond, just a few blocks from our new home. Ukrops would ultimately expand to 29 grocery stores in Richmond and Central Virginia. They would lead the market share for years despite many national contenders trying to take it from them. This was a testament to the family's work ethic and values as they were closed on Sundays and didn't sell alcohol. To this day, the Ukrops are a well-respected and community minded family in Richmond.

We soon met two more neighbors from across the street-a white woman and a black woman. They lived next door to each other and had a morning routine of praying together in one another's home. They told us that one day they had walked around our property and prayed specifically for a Christian family to move in. This was incredibly comforting. As exciting as this adventure was, I still had some apprehension of being in a very different environment. In some ways, it was like my childhood move, but in reverse. I knew no one and was stepping into a culture that was foreign to me. While sensing a call to move into a black neighborhood and trying to imagine what it might be like, I now live here. Thanks to the Hand of Providence that we had witnessed in these past few months and knowing that our new neighbors had been praying for us, we felt a deep sense of peace that we were home.

Yet the journey was only beginning-a journey into our own naivety. We had no idea what lessons lay before us. We had little insight into the historical depths of segregation and the mistrust that permeated the black community. We knew these things existed in the white community, but having spent little time cross-culturally, we had no idea what we were walking into.

Not long after moving in, I was out in the front yard one night when I heard a couple of gunshots followed by several others. I grabbed my keys, jumped in our mini-van, and drove in the direction of the sounds. About a mile up the road was George Wythe High School. As I drew near, there were lots of blue lights flashing and I saw a large crowd gathered outside the gymnasium. I pulled over to the curb and parked. There was a flurry of activity as children and adults quickly moved about. There were many onlookers at this point, standing at a distance and trying to make sense of what was going on. After a few minutes, I got the nerve to get out of the van. I ventured over to someone standing nearby and asked him if he knew what was going on. He said there had been a fight between a couple of students at the basketball game and then they started shooting. I later found out that one of the students had been hit and suffered a minor leg injury. Thank God it was only one student and a minor injury.

This incident certainly made my adrenalin pump as I suddenly found myself witnessing the reality of urban life up close. What a stark contrast to what I had been used to in our suburban and country life. The only gunfire I ever heard there was the occasional early morning or evening shotgun blast aimed at an unsuspecting deer. Prior to moving, I had read accounts of violence in the city from the newspaper. Our local paper, the Richmond Times-Dispatch, carried frequent stories of shootings. There were certain street names that seemed to appear time and time again. It was as if they were a magnet for violence. When I would read these names in the paper, I often wondered where they were. It didn't take long to realize that several of them were within a few blocks of where we had just moved. Some of my other naivety would take a bit longer to surface.

Like the formation of prejudice that I spoke of in the last chapter, our naivety is also affected to varying degrees through our upbringing. According to Merriam-Webster, naivety is defined as "simply having or showing a lack of experience or knowledge." This certainly described us as we began to immerse ourselves cross-culturally. Not just racially, but also economically. And we would come to see just how different each community was. *A Framework for Understanding Poverty* by Dr. Ruby Payne gives some helpful insight into the disparity found in the varying economic classes. The book explores the different mindsets of people living in poverty, the middle-class, and the wealthy. She speaks of unspoken or hidden rules that are generally at play in each of these classes in our society. For example, when it comes to money, those in poverty see it as something to be used and spent. The middle-class view it as something to be managed. Wealthy individuals tend to see money as something to be conserved and invested in to create more wealth.

Apart from the economic class difference that we were stepping into, there was also the cross-racial bridging to navigate. Even though racial segregation has not been legal for many years, it's practical existence in communities is still very much a reality. We moved from a white, middle-class neighborhood in Hanover County to a black, low-economic neighborhood in Richmond City. When people exist in a segregated society for hundreds of years, different world views and ways of navigating life become firmly established. We are often so immersed in our own culture that we have little understanding about the history of another culture. This lack of knowledge can lead to misunderstanding, prejudice, and a lack of empathy toward others. In general, people have a propensity to associate with those who are most like them. Therefore, they are less informed (blind, if you will) of people from a different race. This is the naivety of which I speak.

I believe we can gain some insight into the pervasive nature of naivety by looking more closely at other cultural differences. A few years back, I was asked to serve on the regional leadership team of our denomination, The Association of Vineyard Churches. I was an Area Leader, responsible for the pastoral care of several churches in Virginia and Maryland. This involved interacting with leaders from the cold climate of New England. When our team would get together, we often met in New York, New Jersey or Maine. We typically gathered in the fall for a few days where we would catch up on how we were personally doing and share about the health of the churches we were giving pastoral care to. We'd also have some leadership training and plan our bi-annual regional conference.

The first few meetings I attended were a little intimidating. Twenty of us would be sitting around a table trying to decide on the theme of the conference, its location, or which keynote speaker or worship leader to invite. The conversation at times could be fast and furious, with people jumping in at any moment sharing thoughts and opinions, challenging others and shooting down ideas. There I was trying to make sense of what seemed rude to me at times. When I had something to say, I would politely raise my hand. Suddenly, it would get quiet as all eyes were intently fixed on me with the look of, *what does Ken have to say?*

It was at one of these gatherings that one of the leaders gave me a copy of Sarah Lanier's book, *Foreign to Familiar.* It discusses different ways that people from warm climates and cold climates relate to one another. People from cold climates, when focused on a task, tend to be more direct and to the point. They don't necessarily have any emotion attached to it. Conversely, someone from a warm climate like Virginia would be equally, if not more concerned with the emotions of the person.

The women and men from the northern states were not rude; they were simply focused on the task at hand. There was no thought of offending anyone. On the other hand, I, as a warm-climate southerner, might be described as the proverbial "southern-gentleman" in this situation. It had a lot to do with the culture I was raised in. This was quite an education for this southern, warm-climate introvert. I came to love and truly appreciate these people. I just didn't understand them at first. I believe my northern, "Yankee" friend observed this in me and handed me the book out of kindness.

While my naivety with my cold-climate peers is a bit embarrassing to recall, it provided a lesson that has helped me not to be so quick to judge others who I may not understand, especially those from a culture I have had very little exposure to. I would have many lessons to learn in this regard as it relates to black culture. My naivety would be on full display shortly after we moved into our new neighborhood.

Within a few days of arriving, our next-door neighbor, Ricky, came over to introduce himself. Ricky was a black man who had grown up next door with his brothers. He would go on to shift many of my naïve racial paradigms and stereotypes.

One beautiful spring day, a few months after moving in, I was washing our van in the backyard. We had a nice asphalt driveway that was accessed by an alley that separated our home from Ricky's. Most every day you could find him in his garage preparing a car to be painted, which was his primary job and love. His impressive car detailing skills were a source of great pride for him, and he was good at it. He was never short of work as his custom paint skills were highly sought out. He frequently had friends stopping by to check on their vehicle, but often to just chill. Hearty laughter would often make its way across the alley as Ricky and his friends hung out in his garage.

In my early conversations with Ricky, he was intrigued, but probably more mystified, that we had chosen to move into this part of the city. I remember him saying to me, "I'm trying to get out of the city!" He had a dream to own a house in the country with a big garden and plenty of room for his dog to run. He was curious as to why we would choose to move where we did. He would share with me stories of things he had witnessed while growing up there. He told me about the time he came home one day to find a dead body in their front yard. I didn't get all the details but was just thankful that it had been a few years back. He also spoke of the challenge of petty crimes like theft that were common in the neighborhood.

I gathered that he wanted more of a quiet space than the city offered, so he couldn't fathom why we would give that up by moving where we did. He genuinely welcomed us, and he proved to be one of the kindest and most thoughtful neighbors we've ever had. One of my first memories was how excited he was to bring over his newborn son and show him off to us. He also made it a point to let me know that we didn't really have to worry about anyone messing with us from the alley because he was always there. We were grateful. Little did we know that he truly was our rear security system in those early days as we were oblivious to the crimes that were common in the area.

Ricky also loved music. There were always tunes making their way across the alley expressing much of his personality. On this particular day, as I was washing the van, I noticed he was playing country music. When I became aware of the genre and the volume at which it was being played, I thought to myself, *Ricky really is kind. He knows I'm out here working and he's playing country music on my behalf, knowing I'm from the country.* Did I mention that I was naive? What I eventually discovered was that Ricky really loved country music. And I generally didn't associate black people with country music. It wasn't so much a conscious thought as it was that implicit bias I spoke of in the previous chapter. I feel embarrassed sharing this story; however, it was an early step in my journey over the bridge-a step where my eyes were beginning to see an individual (Ricky) rather than a people group (the black community). Until now, this was a community in which I had spent very little time throughout my life.

Over the years, Ricky became a true friend of the family. He would always bring us thoughtful gifts after he returned from trips. He remembered our children's birthdays. He taught one of our son's basic auto mechanics along with a love for Coca-Cola memorabilia. And he finally purchased that home in the country. It was a sad day when he left, but I was excited that he was able to see this dream become reality. He was happy.

My last memory of Ricky is from an August evening in 2012. He was dancing at our son's wedding reception and having a blast. At the end of the night, he told me what a great time he had. A few short days later, I was walking down the sidewalk near our house when one of his brothers got my attention and called me over. I was shocked to learn that Ricky had just been found dead from a heart attack in his new home. I am grateful that he was finally able to have a place in the country, at least for a little while. I am more grateful, however, that we had the time we had with him. He was a great neighbor and friend. I'm a better person for knowing him.

Ricky was a fixture in the neighborhood and is greatly missed

Ricky having a blast at our son's wedding

If Ricky's love of country music was one of those "aha" moments, our racial education was only just beginning. Are you ready for some hoops?

Chapter 3

We're Ballin' Now

While living in Hanover, one of my favorite pastimes was shooting hoops with my children. Sadly, we had to leave our basketball goal behind when we moved because the pole was cemented in the ground. A few months after arriving in the city, as the weather was starting to warm, I erected a new one next to our paved driveway in the backyard. This had been a Christmas gift for our children, and they had been after me to put it up. I was also looking forward to some quality time with them and the exercise wouldn't hurt either. Little did I know that this simple act of firmly planting a metal pole into the ground was also cementing the foundation of a local community center in our backyard.

I came home from the office one day and found my children playing ball with some neighborhood kids I had yet to meet. It didn't take very long for three or four kids to turn into ten or twelve. This soon became a daily occurrence. Where did they come from? Well, we had made the conscious decision of not putting up a fence when we moved in. We wanted to be intentional about building bridges and not isolating ourselves in the community. This allowed easy access to the court through the alley and the front yard. The constant sound of a basketball bouncing on the pavement was a clarion call that made its way through the neighborhood, not unlike a church bell calling parishioners to worship.

Most of the kids were elementary and middle school age, but it was not unusual for a two-year-old sibling or cousin to be along for the ride. Then, there were the occasional older teens who wanted to come in and dominate the court time. They were a little more challenging for me to interreact with as some of them carried a pretty tough persona. I would join them from time to time, bringing all my 40-something skills to bear. In hindsight, I'm sure I looked and acted pretty goofy at times.

This sudden flurry of activity now happening in our backyard was exciting. We were intrigued by witnessing up close, a slice of culture that was unfamiliar to us. We were also a bit overwhelmed. The continual BOUNCE, BOUNCE, BOUNCE, BOUNCE of the ball, the free-flowing colorful language, the frequent use of the n-word, the in-your-face exposure of underwear rising above sagging pants, the arguments and occasional fights, along with our dog Rascal loudly expressing his opinion, proved to be quite challenging for us.

This would become a daily occurrence, and it didn't take long for our backyard to become the neighborhood playground. As soon as the children came home from school in the afternoon, they would make their way to our house. Occasionally, they would arrive before our own children. Sometimes we'd come home from an outing with our children only to find the backyard already filled with activity.

A typical day on the court

Not everyone was happy about this. I came home one day to find two police officers next door talking to one of our neighbors. She called them to complain. The officers asked if I could move the court to the other side of the yard. I didn't want to do that since we had the pavement of the driveway for the court. We compromised on making sure the kids were only there when we were there, which of course we wanted as well. We also wanted to be good neighbors.

Some days I'd come home from work and be thrilled to see all the activity only to find that Becky had been enduring it for the previous several hours. The novelty of this new urban experience was starting to wear out its welcome, and we knew we had to get a handle on it. At the same time these kids were growing on us.

I decided to establish a few ground rules. I wanted to keep them simple enough to remember, but significant enough to keep some sense of order. I settled on the following:

1. Ask permission before playing.

2. No fighting.

3. No cussing, including the N-word.

4. No sagging (of pants)

And most importantly,

5. HAVE FUN!

I took the time to go over the list with our guests for several days in a row since it was common to have new kids showing up on any given day. One afternoon as I started to list the rules for a new kid, one of our regulars interrupted me and proceeded to explain them to him. I smiled. Later, I would often overhear the veterans explaining the rules to new arrivals without them knowing I was ease-dropping. I smiled again. This did my heart good.

While this might seem like it's settling into a nice little community basketball program, it was more like semi-organized chaos. I soon realized that while some of these kids had a parent or grandparent that had instilled some healthy values and manners in them, there were other kids who seemed to be raising themselves, often with little moral compass. They seemed destined for trouble. When they would toss their jacket, hoodie or backpack to the side of the court to play, I often wondered what might be inside. I'm not sure I really wanted to know.

As you can imagine, we were in uncharted territory again. We entered this new world of urban life by faith, bringing with us all the naivety you might expect. Yet, we had an abiding sense that we were on some kind of divine adventure.

I'll never forget an encounter I had with one of the kids shortly after we moved in. He was around 14 years old and had been ballin' for quite a while one afternoon. He gathered his stuff to leave and started around the front of the house to head up the street. I walked with him a bit, just to be sure he wasn't helping himself to something of ours along the way. As he started to walk off, he looked back at me and said, "Don't worry Mr. Peters. We've got your back."

At the time, I didn't appreciate the significance of that statement. It would be some time before I realized what he was saying. In essence, we had earned his and many of the other kids' respect and they would be looking out for us, protecting us from those who might want to take advantage. This proved true over the years as we had very little issue with theft or vandalism. While I'm sure some of these kids were not respecting other people's property, they respected ours.

Who knew that a $200 basketball goal and a little patience (well, maybe a lot of patience) would turn out to be such a valuable insurance policy? Although, if we look a little deeper, we might find that the real insurance came from our genuine love and respect for the kids, recognizing that each one was made in God's image, the *Imago Dei*.

This truth was brought home to me one day in an unusual way. One of my kids came running into the house telling me that somebody had said something ugly to our oldest daughter who was seventeen at the time. I came out the back door and interrupted the basketball game that was currently happening. I pointed to the fifteen-year-old boy and shouted, "Come with me!" I was mad and he knew it. He followed me around the side of the house toward the front yard. I wanted to let him know that he had better not ever talk to my daughter like that again. I was going to put the fear of God in him. I was ready to tell him to leave and never come back. As we approached the front of the house, the things I had wanted to say, that I had prepared to say, surprisingly changed to, "God really loves you. He has an awesome plan for your life." He looked up at me with an expression on his face that conveyed great confusion. I ended it with something like, "You really should respect women. God loves and respects them, too." He didn't really have anything to say, but from that day forward I noticed a change in the way he interacted with me and my kids.

Talk about flying by the seat of your pants. I believe this is often what a walk of faith looks like. We get a glimpse of the big picture-a sense of God's heart and invitation and we take a step towards it. It's kind of like God saying, "Hold on to your pants. We're going somewhere."

As we step out on this bridge of love, where we intentionally move toward reconciliation by entering the life of someone different from us, we position ourselves for growth. It's here that we have some of our paradigms challenged, but even more importantly, we gain insight into ourselves and our own hearts. It's where our prejudice and biases are exposed and we have the opportunity to align our heart with God's heart.

Having my heart exposed wasn't something I signed up for or expected. Coming into the city, I felt like I had dealt with a lot of my stuff. I had rejected prejudice. I was being intentional in walking the other way, embracing people of color. One of my hopes moving into this community was that our children would grow up free of the prejudice I was raised in. It was during this intentional integration of our family with the black community that my eyes would be opened in ways I never anticipated.

Let me share with you three aha moments that have impacted my heart and become foundational in moving me toward this worthwhile goal of reconciliation.

First, I began to see individuals rather than just a bunch of kids. Now, there are times when it's appropriate to speak about demographics and statistics. For example, when speaking of the percentage of black males incarcerated as related to their percentage of the U.S. population, it can help shine the light on a systemic issue that needs attention. However, there is an inherent danger in this as well. When we only speak of a racial group in some category (black males), the individuals (Jamale, for example) who make up that category often remain invisible. This keeps us at a distance from the reality of the individual's unique challenges and hopes. We can become numb or cynical because we are so far removed from the actual person.

When I hear arguments and debates over racial issues on the news or through social media, too often what I hear are generalizations or abstract scenarios. Phrases like the *inner city, under-served, urban blight,* and *welfare recipients* are often used when referring to the economically poor and people of color. We describe our fellow humans with words like *delinquents, drug dealers, thugs, inmates, offenders, blacks* or perhaps, *the poor.* We hear things like, "the African-American unemployment rate is at an all-time low or an all-time high."

Rarely, when discussing these issues, are we thinking of individuals that we may have met or befriended. Perhaps it's someone who has applied for a job but is not sure how he will get there because he doesn't have transportation. When we draw near to a human being of a different race or culture, the tone and topic of conversation often change for the better. And this change most always affects our heart. When our hearts are affected, we just may be moved to make a difference in someone's life trajectory.

I'm not sure when it first happened, but somewhere along the way, I began to see individuals rather than groups of people. When the kids first showed up in our backyard, my initial perspective was that I was seeing a bunch of black kids. After a while, things changed. I'd look out the window and see Anthony, Aaron, Rodney, Devon, Emanuel, Pooty, Matthew, and Foo Foo. Often, I would find myself saying, "Hey. Who's the new kid?" Then, I would head outside to introduce myself.

As I came to know some of their stories, my heart began to break for these children. I began to sense a love in my heart growing. It's hard to put my finger on how or why it was happening. It wasn't that they were orphans or abused or neglected or that they were unwanted or unloved. Although I was certainly concerned with the well-being of some, I know most of them had families that dearly loved and cherished them. But, as my eyes were opened further to some of the challenges these families faced, I began to have a deepening compassion for them.

As relationships and trust began to be built with some of the children, conversations would open. It was here that I experienced a second aha moment. I came to understand that there were literally dozens of children within walking distance of our house who were labeled "fatherless" for all intent and purposes.

This idea of black fatherlessness has been in the American social conversation for many years. A report was published in 1965 by Senator Patrick Moynihan during the Lyndon Johnson administration that stated how the black family was disintegrating with fatherlessness being a leading factor. This report was controversial as it was perceived by some as blaming the victims. It certainly painted a broad-brushed picture in the minds and hearts of the white community as segregation was still very much a reality during this time.

But the understanding of black fatherlessness hasn't just been a theme in the white community. This message was reinforced through the likes of Bill Cosby and Sidney Poitier. And, on Father's Day, 2008, Senator Barack Obama, gave a speech to the parishioners of a Chicago Church. He basically told them that black men need to grow up and stop using past injustices as an excuse for shirking their responsibilities. During his speech, he said, "Any fool can have a baby." Much of the black church cheered.

Prior to moving into the city, I had heard stories and statistics of absent fathers in the black community and the destructive nature it had left on the family. Again, statistics carry with them an inherent danger, and there has been some legitimate pushback against this idea of fatherlessness in the black community. It has even been referred to as a myth.

To the idea of fatherlessness being a myth, I will give some pushback as well, alongside respect and acknowledgment of my own white bias, or blindness.

My son's good friend lived in public housing on the street behind us. He was at our house practically every day. He would go to church with us most weekends. One Sunday, he was anxious to get home from church because his father was coming to pick him up. I would find out later from my son that his father never showed up. I watched this rejection happen to him repeatedly. I don't know the reason for him not showing, only the disappointment in this young boy's heart.

On another occasion, I went to pick up a teenage boy from his grandmother's house to take him to church. She said he wasn't coming that day because his dad was supposed to come and pick him up. But then she added, "He probably won't show. He usually doesn't." Again, I don't know the reason behind this situation, but the pain for this young teen is real and deep.

Even as I write this, I know there will be some who'll say, "I lost my father at an early age, and I've turned out alright. I'm successful. I got past it. Life's hard for everybody." I believe in the resilience of the human spirit through God's grace. I know both boys by name and there is hope for them, but it doesn't just happen.

After living in this community for twenty plus years, I discovered that there is a difference. When we were hosting a reading club in our home a few years back, the pervasiveness of this issue became apparent. Early on, we had around twenty-five children who regularly attended. I noticed that I was only interacting with the mothers and grandmothers of the children. When I inquired a bit further, I found that only one of the families had a father living in the home, and he was their stepfather. Can you see how an entire community might be affected by this void found in so many homes?

I am aware of how this may come across as broad-brushing or stereotypical. How can I express the pain I have witnessed time and time again in young boys' and girls' hearts without appearing to condemn a large swath of black men? That is the last thing I want to do.

I have also witnessed black fathers who have been present in their children's lives-who walked their children to school and later to our reading club. Honestly, I am amazed at the resilience I've witnessed in many black men who have had to navigate a plethora of systemic injustices that would cause many a man to give up. I've witnessed the love of a father toward his children and seen the ache in his heart that he couldn't do more for them.

I am simply speaking from my own observations and experience with those who have crossed my path. Just like any ethnic group, there is no homogeneous equity or experience. There are great fathers in every race and there are absent fathers in every race. However, there are unique systemic issues facing the black community that I have seen up close. They have had, in my opinion, a deep, lasting pernicious effect on the family. It's these heartbreaking effects that move me to challenge this idea of myth. One these systemic issues is the mass incarceration of black males. While I won't attempt to unpack this issue here, it has been covered thoroughly by Michelle Alexander in her book, *The New Jim Crow*. However, I will share an experience that brought it home for me a few years back.

While pastoring our church, I was also bi-vocational for several years, working as a mobile x-ray technologist. Mobile x-ray is used for folks when it is difficult for them to get to a medical facility for basic x-ray exams. My job took me into nursing homes, private homes, and correctional facilities. One day I was in our local city jail waiting for a patient to arrive. The room, where we performed the exams, opened into a hallway that led to the cafeteria. As I stood scanning the hallway awaiting the arrival of my patient, I was drawn to an image that haunts me to this day. There was a line of mostly young black males as far as I could see walking slowly toward the cafeteria. After they made their way in, another line took their place, again with only young black males. And then, another line. I was overwhelmed by the sight. I'm looking around at the guards and other employees thinking to myself. *Does everybody see what I'm seeing? How can this be? Something is desperately wrong.*

One day, as I was once again standing at the doorway observing the cafeteria scene, I heard a voice say, "Hey, Mr. Peters." I scanned the line and asked who said that. While keeping a wary eye on the guard, a young black man acknowledge it was him. I didn't recognize him. He said, "I used to come over to your house and play basketball." My heart broke. How many kids have passed through our lives? Where are they now?

As I sit writing this, another young man whom I know is currently in that cafeteria line. He's just nineteen. I first met him when he was around eight years old. He was riding his bike with some friends one day. As they passed our house, his chain came off and he asked me if I could fix it. Over the next few years, I would get to know him and the rest of his family. To me, he's still that kid. Only now, he's followed his father's footsteps into the criminal justice system. Where will it end? When will it end?

It dawns on me that fatherless children and that long line of young black men have a correlation. Many of these young men are hardly out of their adolescent and teenage years and are now fathers themselves, their children being primarily raised by their mothers.

One other piece of this aha moment was that while I was mostly aware of the young black males suffering from fatherlessness, I began to wonder how this was affecting the girls as well? It wasn't until some of them began attending our reading club did the scope of the fatherlessness of young black females begin to hit me. Perhaps it was my own gender bias that obscured their pain from me initially, but it's no less devastating. In some ways it's created an even greater vulnerability for them.

The third aha moment is perhaps the hardest one to acknowledge. It's the fear of letting someone have a piece of my heart. There was a kid who began to spend more time with us. He was someone who didn't have a relationship with his biological father and was longing for that connection. Although he probably wasn't fully aware of it or able to articulate it, from our vantage point, it was obvious. He spent a lot of time with us having meals in our home, spending the night, and essentially becoming part of our family.

His mom suffered some serious health issues. One night, I received a phone call from her asking me if we would consider raising him if anything ever happened to her. We, of course, told her yes. Then, at some point, this kid began to call Becky, Mama. She readily embraced this. She had already given him her heart. When he made similar overtures toward me, kind of testing the waters a bit, suddenly I was exposed. Could I let my heart go there? After all, he wasn't really my child, my flesh and blood. It scared me to think of giving myself away like that and it exposed my heart and perhaps even my motives. It set me on a course of examining myself and caused me to lean into my faith and ask some hard questions.

As someone who purported to follow Jesus, shouldn't I be doing what he did? His heart was already given to this young boy. What was holding me back? I hadn't yet followed Him to this place. One day I was in prayer, talking with God about this dilemma. I asked God to help me. Let's just say, He is proving Himself faithful as I have seen some of the defensive walls around my heart begin to crumble. This is a difficult and embarrassing reality to admit. Yet, as I've allowed myself to be vulnerable, I've witnessed my heart expand. I think that's how it happens.

As you and I step across this bridge of love, of God's heart, and into the lives of those different from us, our hearts will be exposed and challenged. This can be frightening initially, but if we're willing to trust our hearts to the One who made them and is forming them, there is a softening that awaits.

I take that step across that bridge of vulnerability because I know that Jesus awaits me on the other side and that it's His Love that invites me to step out in faith. The result has been a life of adventure unlike anything I could have ever imagined and a journey of discovering my true self. By putting myself in uncomfortable and challenging situations, I have learned things about myself and others that I could never have learned otherwise. Even more importantly, I've come to experience the incredible Faithfulness of God and His relentless love for these children.

Now, I realize that you will most likely never find yourself moving into a neighborhood like our family did, but the principle still applies. We can all step out of our comfort zone and cross the bridge of love and step into someone's life that up until now has been kept at a safe distance. It may be someone you work with, perhaps in the next office or cubicle. It may be a neighbor, a classmate, or a teammate. It might even be a new family member. Ask them out for lunch or coffee. Be curious. Ask them about their life, their family and really listen. You will discover that stereotypes you may have had will begin to lose some of their power. You will see one person rather than just another group of people. You'll see someone with hopes, dreams, and struggles just like you.

Most importantly, you will likely discover thoughts and attitudes within yourself that you never knew existed. This is the generational prejudice or implicit bias that is a part of all of us. I believe that until we acknowledge this and begin to intentionally take steps away from it, there is little hope for true reconciliation in our personal relationships or for our nation. This I believe is the crux of the matter. If we allow ourselves the grace and time to acknowledge our biases and begin to turn from them, a whole new world will open to us and to others. At the very least it creates the potential for something beautiful and redemptive.

Chapter 4

The Plank Eye

Since we were moving in the middle of the school year, one of the major decisions we had to make rather quickly was where to send our children to school. Our oldest daughter was allowed to complete her senior year at the county school she attended. Our other children would be changing schools. We felt that if we were going to be authentic to our values and desire for racial reconciliation, then our kids needed to attend school in the zone in which we lived. Our journey into the inner-city public school system was about to begin. And what an education it would be for all of us.

For our middle school daughter, this turned out to be an experience that would prove quite challenging. She was just getting acclimated to her first year of middle-school when she had to leave her school and life-long friends behind. She soon found herself riding a city school bus filled with kids from a very different demographic. She caught the bus a block away from our home at a corner that served as a drive-thru drug market from late afternoon until early morning.

Was this decision reckless or irresponsible? To this day, I'm not sure how to process that, other than to say we felt that this was the right thing to do. There were many other parents in our neighborhood who sent their kids to the same bus stop. There was no other choice for them. How could we use our privilege of transportation while others didn't have that option? And, while my daughter has become a strong, resilient and kind woman, I wish I had been more attuned to what she was experiencing daily. Middle school is a tough enough adjustment, let alone being tossed into a foreign environment, often feeling alone and vulnerable.

As for our three younger children, they attended Patrick Henry Elementary School which was two blocks up the street from us. At that time, the school's demographic was nearly 100% black. Our family created quite a contrast. Prior to putting them in school, Becky and I met with the principal. She was a Godly woman who truly loved the children under her watch. She put us at ease as she shared her faith with us and her devotion to the students. We felt very comfortable enrolling our children.

Our four-year-old daughter was placed in the early childhood program at Patrick Henry with a wonderful and most beloved teacher, Mr. Edwards. He exuded love for the children. I'll never forget the day she came home from school and told us that the kids in her class kept rubbing her hair. We asked her why they were doing that. She didn't know. We would later learn that her classmates wanted to know what a white person's hair felt like, so in their curiosity, they rubbed her long straight blond hair. This innocent little gesture by the black children in our daughter's class gave us a glimpse into the "great divide" that was still alive and well in Richmond, Virginia.

Our two boys were in first and third grade and were creating quite the contrast as well. One February, at a PTA meeting, my younger son's class was doing a recitation of a poem for Black History Month. It was *The Weary Blues* by renowned African-American poet, Langston Hughes.

Maggie feeling right at home

Here's our blond haired, blue-eyed son surrounded by a sea of black haired, brown-eyed children swaying back and forth in rhythm saying;

"The night is beautiful,
So the faces of my people.
The stars are beautiful,
So the eyes of my people.
Beautiful, also, is the sun.
Beautiful, also, are the souls of my people."

Just picture that for a moment. To this day, I regret not having my camera with me. I would have captured that precious moment. It's still a memory I will carry with me for the rest of my life. In some ways it was the snapshot of our journey into black America.

Our oldest son was quick to make friends and fit right in. He's that kid in the grocery cart at the store that waves and says hi to everyone he passes along the way. To this day, if there's another human being around, he'll find a way to talk with them. He was in an all-boys class of combined grades called, Boys to Men. It was taught by an incredible educator named Gregory Stallings. My son thrived under his tutelage.

For the most part, we were warmly welcomed by the school staff and other families despite the anomaly that we were. After settling in, attending school functions and your typical PTA meetings, I began to sense something that I had never experienced before. I felt myself getting the cold shoulder from other parents. It dawned on me that I was being confronted with something I had never known before. I was experiencing prejudice because I was a white person. I could never remember feeling that level of isolation, judgement and condescension from anyone simply because of my race. The air was thick with it at times. Then I had a revelation. This is what the black community had experienced from the white community for years. I felt sick about it and instantly felt regret ever causing another person to feel what I was feeling in that moment. I am grateful for this experience because it helps me to be more sensitive to this prejudice that lies within. It helps inform my intentionality of being inclusive and welcoming to black people that I meet for the first time.

One thing we did have a clue about, thanks to some practical teaching on race relations by the likes of Wellington Boone and John Dawson, was to be sensitive about coming into a black environment and exercising our white privilege. I don't recall them using that language back in the 90's, but it was the same idea. We were intentional about coming in and looking for ways to serve in the school, not trying to change anything. Even saying that demonstrates how blind we (whites) sometimes are to our own biases. We just know the way things should be done-at least that's the way we've always done them. We avoided talking about our experiences in Hanover County Public Schools. Yet, despite our reluctance toward any place of position, it didn't take long for us to be invited into the PTA and then nominated for office. As anyone working in most public-school systems know, just a warm body will often do. We were available and willing to serve.

In our second year, I was elected Vice-President and Becky, Chaplain. Yes, the PTA in this public school had an Office of Chaplain. This was another moment of enlightenment for us. Faith expressed in this inner-city school was not something that was considered politically incorrect. Rather, it was simply an expression of an integral part of life for many black families. Scripture was referenced by the principal in the PTA meetings without a second thought in the natural flow of conversation. This was quite refreshing in contrast to the inhibition that is often felt by people who genuinely walk by faith. Faith has been a source of strength in the black community for generations, a sustaining hope during great pain and struggle. So, it was quite natural for the female black principal to include it in her addresses at the meetings.

After a year of serving in this capacity, I was elected president of the PTA board. I felt very inadequate in this position yet honored that these folks of another race would consider me for this important position. Perhaps they were less concerned about the racial issue than I was at the time. We never talked about it. Most people tend to guard their innermost thoughts and motives, particularly when it comes to racial issues. Yet sometimes we let our guard down and the potential for offense occurs.

One afternoon, after wrapping up a PTA board meeting, a few of us were milling around, talking before we left. I was the only white person in the room and while I'm talking with another member, a couple of ladies were carrying on a conversation next to us. They were talking at a volume that made it hard not to be distracted from my own conversation. I heard one of them tell a white joke, which I had never heard before. Growing up in a prejudicial environment I had heard my share of black jokes, but never a white joke. When the woman telling the joke suddenly realized that I had overheard her, she became extremely embarrassed and said, "Oh, I'm so sorry, Mr. Peters."

As I was trying to process what I was hearing and stumbling all over myself to tell her it was okay, the woman I was speaking with quickly intervened on my behalf and said, "Oh, don't worry about Mr. Peters. He's one of us."

Even though as white man I was the subject of their humor, I felt like I belonged. That we were on this bridge together. What we found at Patrick Henry Elementary was an environment of faith and dedication by the staff, faculty, and parents to a group of children who desperately needed it. The principal. loved the kids and kept extra coats and other clothing items for those who showed up in need. The school welcomed us, loved us and graciously put up with our first staggering steps toward racial reconciliation. I'm sure I said things that were stupid or ignorant. If they noticed, they kept their thoughts to themselves and showed much long-suffering toward this well-intentioned family, albeit novices at this important work.

While we were having such a great experience, I couldn't help but wonder why there weren't more white children attending Patrick Henry. On the opposite side of the school from where we lived was a neighborhood made up of approximately 95% white families, many with school aged children. Where were the white kids? This was their zoned school. We would later learn that families could apply for schools outside of their zone. The public-school buses would come through the neighborhood and pick up the kids and take them *across the water* to other schools that were predominantly white. This was 1998. How could this be? Why was the surrounding white community steering clear of this wonderful neighborhood school?

One evening, I was invited to join a school representative to attend one of the neighborhood community meetings to showcase the school. The goal was to encourage the parents to enroll their children in Patrick Henry. It was within walking distance for most of the families. I'm sure I caused a few heads to tilt when they realized that my kids attended school there. And, while everyone was kind and inclusive at the meeting, we were unsuccessful in our recruitment. It would be nearly a decade before some of the white neighborhood kids attended the school, and this only after the school closed, and a charter school opened in its place. I'm grateful to say that when you look at the school's playground today, there is a beautiful reflection of racial diversity, although gentrification has had a major impact on the surrounding black community.

Before our kids moved on from Patrick Henry, I still had an important lesson to learn. My pride and ignorance needed another unveiling. Two years into our school experience, a new principal arrived. Things changed quickly. While we had really found our groove in the school community and felt totally at home, Becky and I both felt like something had shifted in the school climate. This was also the time that the new state SOL (standards of learning) testing was being implemented. The new principal and her vice-principal were understandably focused on this since it was mandated. However, things were very different from previous leadership. The new principal was outwardly kind to us, but she kept a distance. The new vice-principal tolerated us, at best. We reached out to her, showed her kindness, looked for ways to serve, but didn't feel the same welcome we had received before.

I remember one opportunity that occurred later in the school year that I originally felt was squandered. It was a school day PTA presentation with all the children in the assembly. The meeting took place in February as we celebrated Black History Month. After the children's beautiful and lively presentations, the principal made her way to the podium to address everyone present. She spoke of the many struggles of the black people throughout the years. And then she said, "But we still have a long way to go." I had been sitting next to her throughout the program and thought to myself, why don't you acknowledge me and say something like, "However we're moving in the right direction."

Again, this is where my bias and naivety show. Her focus wasn't on reconciliation, but it was on the systemic injustices that continue to impact black communities across America. She was speaking to the next generation, encouraging them to keep the struggle and fight alive and moving forward. How quick I am to judge others from my very narrow and ill-informed worldview, no matter how much my heart desires justice. I had very little appreciation at the time of this wonderful opportunity afforded me. What a privilege to have this inside glimpse into the formation of the black conscience. The struggle, the injustices, the oppression that black America has experienced and that continues to be a reality was right before my eyes, but my white paradigm had hidden it from my view.

There is a story in the bible where Jesus speaks about how we try to bring a solution to someone's problem, thinking that we know what the answer is and yet our vision is clouded. We aren't really seeing the situation clearly. We end up not helping at all and often causing more harm than good. Jesus put it this way, "Why do you notice the small piece of dust that is in your friend's eye, but you don't notice the big piece of wood that is in your own? Why do you say to your friend, 'Let me take that piece of dust out of your eye'? Look at yourself first. You still have that big piece of wood in your own eye. You are a hypocrite. First, take the wood out of your own eye. Then you will see clearly to get the dust out of your friend's eye."

What great imagery Jesus used. Imagine a person with a literal 2 x 4 sticking out of one of their eyes and coming towards another person to help them get a tiny little speck out of one of their eyes. Even as the person would try to get close, they would end up hitting the other person with the 2 x 4. Now imagine for a minute that these 2 x 4's represent our prejudices, our implicit biases, our narrow way of understanding the world-where we're seeing through the eyes of generational prejudice. Can you see how even with good intentions we might be like a bull in a China shop? I have witnessed this more times than I care to mention.

One observation I've had over the years is that most conversations about race tend to occur when there is some current controversy. Here in Richmond, we've had our share. There was a huge uproar about the placement of a monument to recognize the great humanitarian, tennis star and Richmond native, Arthur Ashe. What was the problem? It was being placed on Richmond's beloved Monument Avenue. Prior to this, the avenue was only home to monuments of several Confederate Generals, Jefferson Davis, the President of the Confederacy and Matthew Fontaine Maury, a Confederate naval officer. But this controversy over Arthur Ashe was nothing compared to the upheaval that took place over the Confederate monuments being dismantled and removed. Lines were drawn in the sand, emotions flared, and ultimately little understanding was accomplished. We can't seem to appreciate our fellow human's point of view because our eyes are clouded by our own generational prejudice.

The racial divide plays out ad nauseum on the network news channels where a host directs questions to people from opposing sides of an issue. One guest will state their opinion along with statistics to shore up their point of view. Then, the opposing guest patiently, or not so patiently, awaits their turn to speak their talking points. Little listening to the other side occurs. Often the result is a shouting match, which accomplishes nothing of substance. We are listening to individuals with planks in their eyes.

Wouldn't our world be a better place if we could humble ourselves enough to see if, as Jesus said, there is a plank in our own eye, the plank of prejudice? If we're willing to remove the plank from our own eye (acknowledge our own prejudice), we would be in a much better position to have constructive dialogue.

After living in the community for several years, we began to have our eyes opened to the many challenges lying before the children on their path to adulthood. Let's take another step across the water.

Chapter 5

The Womb of Injustice

Tap! Tap! Tap! Silence. **Tap! Tap! Tap!** Who could possibly be knocking on our front door at six o'clock on a Monday morning? We had been living here for a few months and only briefly said hello to our neighbors. While I was still in a deep sleep, Becky was already up and into her morning routine of prayer and reading. She made her way to the foyer and peered through the peephole in the door. *Who was this young black boy on our porch? Was he in trouble? Was he lost? Where were his parents?* All these thoughts come rushing to her mind.

Since he didn't seem particularly threatening, Becky opened the door. A little seven-year-old boy looked up at her and asked, "Can you take me to school?" He went on to tell her that he lived down the street and his mother had gone to work. *Was he on his own?* As we would later learn, his mother was working two jobs, going to school part-time, and raising three boys by herself.

Becky asked, "What's your name?" He proudly replied, "Devin." She invited him in and let him lie on the sofa until our other children woke up. After eating breakfast with us, Becky took him to school with our kids. We had no idea that this morning routine would continue through high school.

Why did Devin pick our house, the white family, and the newcomers to the neighborhood? Well, to answer that question, we must rewind to the previous evening. We were at our church for a special meeting with a children's pastor from Rhode Island named Bob Bradbury, or Captain Bob as he was affectionately known. He had been a professional fisherman most of his life and had recently

43

sold his business to travel the world ministering to children. This Sunday night, he captured the attention of all the children present, including my six and eight-year-old sons.

As part of his presentation, Captain Bob handed out index cards to the children and asked them to write down the name of one of their friends. He encouraged them to pray for their friend each night before going to sleep. As I was putting the boys to bed later that evening, we went through our regular ritual of kneeling to pray before climbing into bed. They each pulled out their index cards. When I looked at them, they had both written the name Devin. When I asked them who Devin was, they both said that he was one of the boys who they met in school.

While I can't recall specifically what we prayed for, I suspect it was something along the lines of, "Lord, we lift Devin up to you. We ask that you bless him. And if he doesn't already, may he come to know you for himself."

Little did we know how quickly those prayers would be answered a few short hours later with a tap, tap, tap on our front door. How blessed we would be by him coming into our lives.

It didn't take long for Devin to become one of the family. He was at our house every morning, after school until the streetlights came on, and nearly every weekend. Devin began coming to church with us and soon became a regular member of our congregation. One Christmas for the children's program, he played the part of Joseph in the nativity scene. Everyone loved Devin.

Devin and our daughter as Mary and Joseph in the nativity scene

Several years after that fateful knock on our door, things were about to change. As suddenly as Devin had come into our life, we got the news that he was moving. In the early 2000's, the real estate market was booming in Richmond. Property values were rising throughout the city. By this time, we had grown close to Devin's mother and his two brothers. Their landlord, seeing the potential for more income, raised her rent by $200 a month. She was barely getting by as it was. She decided to move in with her mother in a tiny little house where her sister and her two nieces were already living.

For the next couple of years, Devin found himself sleeping on a mattress on the floor next to his mother's bed. His older brothers had moved in with other relatives. Devin had just entered high school and had shown a real talent for football. He became the starting center for the George Wythe bulldogs. It wasn't too long after moving in with his grandmother that Devin's mom had a stroke and was unable to work at all. This young boy's world, as stable as it was, had just been turned upside down by the often-unseen cost of gentrification.

It was during this time that we got another glimpse into the depths of the racial divide here in our city. Devin was at the house one day and told us about an incident that had caused him to be kicked out of class at school. His history teacher had gone on a lengthy hate-laced tirade about the white schools in the suburbs and how awful white people were in general and how oppressed black people continue to be today. Some truth, yes, but mixed with prejudice and hatred that would create a lasting impression on young minds and hearts.

Devin grew tired of his teacher's rant and finally spoke up and said, "My white parents aren't like that!" What courage it took for him to stand up in his all-black class and challenge the hatred he felt spewing from his teacher. You see, in some unforeseen way, Devin had identified with us. His teacher went on to tell him that if he didn't like it, he could leave. So, he left class and found his football coach and told him what had happened. A few days later his history teacher approached Devin and apologized to him.

What might have been behind this teacher's anger? If we are willing to look past his initial outburst and listen with the intention of understanding, we may get a glimpse into the very real challenges that many in the black community face. The injustices Devin's teacher was trying to communicate to the children he taught had their place in reality. Since moving into the neighborhood, we were beginning to have our eyes opened to some heart-breaking truths. Many of the children growing up here seem to have the deck stacked against them.

Compared to my relatively safe and secure upbringing, these children's lives could be described as anything but safe and secure. It's not just the very real potential for physical harm or incarceration faced by many. It's also the many systemic issues that create obstacles, hindering their ability to reach adulthood in a flourishing manner. I believe an analogy can be instructive here.

In recent years, much emphasis has been placed on prenatal care for expectant mothers. The human womb is designed to be one of the safest and most nurturing environments on the planet. When a pregnant woman is instructed in prenatal care, the desired outcome is a healthy, viable child delivered at full term with the opportunity to flourish. It's been documented that mothers who take good care of themselves during pregnancy greatly enhance these odds. Typical instructions for an expectant mother include good nutrition, exercise, rest, regular ob-gyn appointments, and to avoid tobacco, alcohol, and drugs while keeping stress to a minimum.

I believe this picture of the human womb as a place of physical development can help us understand and appreciate much of the civil unrest we have witnessed in our nation through the years. The depth of our racial divide is continually being revealed. As video images of violent encounters between police officers and black citizens go viral or an unjust verdict is issued from our judicial system, anger erupts. This is often followed by uncomfortable images crossing our television screens of protests, both peaceful and violent. A movement called *Black Lives Matter* has emerged in recent years and proved as divisive as our racial fissure. In response, counter phrases appear, *All Lives Matter, White Lives Matter, Blue Lives Matter* _____ *Lives Matter*, fill in the blank. It's an understandable reaction given our country's racial history. But, as is often the case in our racial monologues, these responses miss the point.

If we can hit the pause button for a moment on our first impressions and visceral reactions, I believe we can begin to understand some of what is behind the anger we have witnessed and hopefully move toward more constructive dialogue and conciliation. You see, there is another womb-the womb of the inner city. This is a womb where thousands of children find themselves today. Through no choice of their own, they are growing up in a toxic environment that threatens their ability to emerge into adulthood as physically, emotionally and mentally healthy human beings.

Some children find their young lives exposed to violence on a regular basis. I know one young boy who has experienced this violence up close. He saw his stepfather lying dead in the parking lot of his apartment moments after being shot. Two years later, he's running from bullets flying as a family friend is hit and killed right behind him at a community picnic. He is a kind and sensitive boy but has experienced a great deal of trauma at a very young age. *Will he flourish in adulthood? Will he make it to adulthood?*

As I've stated before, many of the children who have crossed our path have absent fathers, some of whom are incarcerated or dead. Most are being raised in single-parent homes. They are impacted by poor nutrition and real hunger, often because of limited access to grocers with healthier options. Lack of affordable housing leads to multiple relocations by families. Many students are passed through the public school system reading well below grade level. If that isn't enough, they are often judged on how they handle these enormous challenges of trauma. Tragically, some do not make it to adulthood at all.

There has been some wonderfully enlightening research done in recent years by the Center for Disease Control. There's a study called the CDC-Kaiser Adverse Childhood Experiences Study. Adverse Childhood Experiences (ACE's) are serious childhood traumas that result in toxic stress that can harm a child's brain. This toxic stress may prevent a child from learning, from playing in a healthy way with other children, and can result in long-term health problems. There is a 10-question survey that can be administered to determine an ACE score. The topics cover emotional, physical or sexual abuse, emotional or physical neglect, parental separation or divorce, domestic violence, substance abuse in family, mentally ill family members and incarcerated family members. Someone with an ACE score of 6 or higher may have their lifespan shortened by 20 years. Many, if not most of the children we have known, would receive an ACE score of 4 or higher. I know several children who are 6 and some even as high as 10. It doesn't have to be this way.

There was another study done by Virginia Commonwealth University that examined life expectancies in different neighborhoods in Richmond. They found a lifespan difference of 14 years between two neighborhoods (Westover

Hills and Swansboro) that were less than a mile apart. They discovered a 20-year difference between one neighborhood (Westover Hills) and one of the public housing projects (Gilpin Court). This study also looked at the connection between neighborhood conditions and health. For example, some reasons given for the disparity in health included the following: education, unsafe or unhealthy housing, opportunities for residents to exercise, walk, or cycle, proximity to highways, access to primary care doctors and good hospitals, unreliable or expensive public transit and residential segregation.

Perhaps this is a good place to hit the pause button again. The information I just shared above is a lot to take in. Unfortunately, it's easy to read past this grouping of issues without recognizing the impact any one of them may have on a child. And, if we're viewing this from a distance, we might be tempted to think that with just a little more effort they can have the same freedoms and opportunities afforded to every American citizen. It's simply not true. Perhaps we affix blame on the parents and in some cases, rightly so. You might be surprised, though, at the level of love and support faithfully present in the parents of many of these children, wanting the best for them, yet working as if they have one arm tied behind their back.

In my opinion, it's only by the grace of God and an incredible tenacity and faithfulness forged in the fires of adversity that help deliver these children into adulthood and some on to success. Even when I have a hard time seeing past some of the self-inflicted situations the parents find themselves in, I try to pause for a moment and consider the children. They are the ones who have no choice in their environment. They are simply recipients of another's choice and might I add, enabled by our society's years of turning a blind eye. I call this "the womb of injustice."

What might be the crucial ingredient in helping us move toward a society where justice is a reality? Instead of judging a group of people from a distance, what if we were to connect with someone outside of our regular circle and learn more about them? Perhaps then, we might come to understand Father Gregory Boyle's advice. "Here is what we seek: a compassion that can stand in awe at what the poor have to carry rather than stand in judgment at how they carry it."

I think of a story of a young man who used to play basketball in our backyard when he was a kid. He's a young father now and had just walked his two young daughters several blocks to the Wednesday reading club that we had started in our home for neighborhood children. When I saw him, a huge smile crossed my face. I was so glad to see him. As he stepped into our noisy, crowded foyer, the first thing I noticed was his long dreadlocks and the pungent aroma of alcohol. After speaking to me for a minute and signing his girls in, he turned to leave. Then he stopped and looked back at me and said, "This is a good thing y'all are doing. We need more of these. You feel me?" I smiled again. Why yes, we do.

We've all heard the adage, *don't judge a book by its cover* because first impressions can be deceiving. This is true in this father's case. Here's a man who loves his children and is trying to do right by them, to give them a bright future. I know that if some of my Caucasian friends were to pass this young father on the sidewalk, they may initially experience a sense of caution or perhaps even fear. How do I know this? I'm that person, too! But these are simply assumptions and stereotypical thoughts. I'd like to think I've moved beyond the prejudicial attitudes and that I have become an enlightened person who has severed all ties to the generational racism of my ancestors. There are times when I may come across that way, and I do believe that I have made progress. However, if I am completely honest, a more apt description would be that I am, at best, a recovering prejudiced person. While I still have a long way to go in this journey of recovery, I have learned a few things along the way.

The next time we cross paths with this father (or someone who looks like him), what if we saw him through the eyes of compassion, that he might be one of these children as well? Could he have grown up in this womb of injustice?

We could simply smile or perhaps speak a word of encouragement and if conversation ensues, listen to him. From this place of empathy, a compassion may emerge, and we just may be moved to action. We may be moved to help remedy a situation, to change a life-trajectory and begin to see justice birthed. We might even find that he has an answer to a problem we've been grappling with.

Imagine a place where the womb of the inner city becomes a healthier, safer environment and its children are born into adulthood with the opportunity to flourish.

In the meantime, what can be done to bring prenatal justice to this womb? We must resist the temptation to think it's beyond hope. We must resist the temptation to think that it's someone else's problem to solve.

If some of these issues sound familiar to you and you are finding your heart moved, then perhaps it's an invitation for you. It might be literacy scores or drop-out rates that move you. Perhaps it's affordable housing that is desperately needed by many. Or maybe it's helping someone struggling with an addiction. Before we throw our hands up and say these issues are bigger than anything I can do, let's see if maybe faith has something to offer us.

Here is an example from the injustice we witnessed with Devin's mother that appeared impossible to remedy. After visiting Devin at his grandmother's house one day, we witnessed his crowed living situation. Becky and I couldn't shake the thought of him living long term in these conditions. We didn't know what we could do about it. We were raising our own large family, yet he was family too, spending most weekends at our home. Becky, being a realtor, was aware of houses on the market in our area. One day, she told me about a house five blocks away that had just come on the market. It was a two-bedroom, one bath home in relatively good condition. We both had the same thought. Wouldn't it be great if Devin and his mom could move back into the neighborhood?

We decided to go for it. Now, keep in mind that we could not afford another mortgage on a house, even if we could get a loan. However, loans were easy to qualify for back in those days. Remember, this was pre-2008 when money was flowing freely in the real estate market. Even so, this was a huge step of faith. We contacted a loan originator and sure enough we could get a loan for it. We had no idea how this was going to work. We only knew that Devin and his family were experiencing an injustice. We went forward with it and secured the loan. The house was ours.

We knew Devin's mom wouldn't be able to buy or rent the house, and we certainly couldn't afford it. We just felt that this was the right thing to do. Keep in mind that we hadn't mentioned anything about what we were doing to anyone, including Devin or his mom. They had no idea. Here is where faith expresses itself.

Two days after we closed on the house, Devin's mom called Becky out of the blue and told her that after a two-year process, she had just gotten approved for Section 8 housing and could Becky help her find a house to rent. In Richmond, while there are several public housing projects and apartments that are considered in Section 8 for rent subsidies, there are also individual houses that can qualify for rental as well. Becky told her what we had just done and that we would figure out the Section 8 process to have the house approved. We had the house inspected, and Devin and his mom moved back into the neighborhood three months later. He now had his own bedroom again. We smiled at the goodness of God and His untiring concern for the children.

One morning, a few days later, and eight years after Devin's initial tap on the door, there was a knock on the front door. Becky opened the door and there stood Devin. He said, "Can you give me a ride up to school?"

He walked a few blocks to the house and wanted a ride the rest of the way to school. Some things never change, like the unchanging faithfulness of God.

I believe with all my heart that God saw Devin and his mom and cared about them even more than we did. He stirred our hearts to act. He was in the details. He provided their need. God has a history of that, and He is inviting you and me into the story of bringing hope to the *womb of injustice.*

Little did we know that God was just getting started with us. He was about to expand our hearts and lives in ways we never saw coming.

Chapter 6

Living the Dream

It began with a dream-a literal dream. There was a box-truck driving fast up our street that looked like a delivery vehicle-the large sliding doors for easy access. The driver was a man who appeared to be in a great hurry, almost as if he was trying to get away from someone. Just as it was passing the front of our house, a young black boy suddenly popped up from the floorboard of the truck. With a terrified expression on his face, he stretched his hand toward me and screamed, "Help us, Mr. Peters!"

I woke up, startled. It was such a vivid and visceral dream that I was shaken by it. I shared it with Becky the next morning. It felt like there was something significant to it, perhaps some kind of divine invitation, toward what though, I wasn't sure, but I started to wonder. I did feel certain that the us the boy spoke of were the children in the neighborhood. How was I supposed to help them? I decided to sit with it for a while. By this time, we had come to know many of the children. And we were aware of the struggles with reading that many of them faced. After a couple of months, an idea came to me. Maybe we could start a reading club. I had no previous experience with teaching literacy, but we could certainly read with some children.

The first thing I did was to reach out to my son's best friend, Matthew. He lived in an apartment on the street behind us. I told him what I had in mind and asked if he knew some kids who might want some help with reading.

He said, "funny you should ask. We just found out that my little brother is reading at kindergarten level."

"What grade is he in?"

He replied, "third."

I said, "well, let's start with him." This short conversation in Matthew's side yard proved to be the foundation of what we would later call, Matthew's Place Reading Club.

The following Wednesday night, Matthew walked his brother over to our house. We ate pizza, read books to him for 30 minutes, then had dessert. We implemented this ritual every Wednesday for the next couple of months. During this period, several people from our church heard what we were doing and decided to join us. We had five adults hovering over this one kid. He loved the attention. It was then that someone suggested we invite more children. Everyone agreed.

Halloween was approaching. We made some invitations for the reading club to distribute to the trick-or-treaters. We set up tables in the front yard and passed out the flyers, along with some really good candy. About 150 children stopped by that night. I'm pretty sure some of them made repeat trips.

When the following Wednesday arrived, our team was really excited about who might show up. There was a palpable sense of anticipation. Our start time approached, and I stood at the front door staring down the street. I was thinking to myself that nobody is going to bring their child to a random white person's house from some flyer they received with their candy. It was then that I noticed two women walking up the city sidewalk along with three children. When they arrived in front of the house, they stopped and looked up at me. Could it be? Was someone really showing up because of our flyers? I was excited. I stepped outside and greeted them. Indeed, they had one of the flyers in hand and proceeded to drop off the children. They had just walked six blocks.

The next week, they came again. I told the grandmother that I would be happy to bring them home, so they didn't have to walk back over. It didn't take long before I picked them up as well. Having four children certainly brought a new dynamic to our club. These new children brought every bit of their active personalities with them. This sometimes made it challenging to move into the dedicated reading time. But, after a few weeks, we settled into a good rhythm.

My grandson and another child reading together

The following spring, we had a few more curious church members stop by. Once again, someone suggested that we could handle a few more children. It seemed like a good idea, but how would we invite more children? We decided to venture out across Midlothian Turnpike which was a couple of blocks away. There was an apartment complex there that we thought might be home to some kids in need of reading help. We made up some more flyers, bought some ice-cream sandwiches and put them on dry ice in a cooler. We loaded the cooler in a wagon and headed out.

As we approached the apartment complex, with our wagon in tow, there was a group of young males standing in front of the buildings. Noticing us, one of the young men walked over to me and asked me what we were doing there. I quickly realized that these guys were working their territory. Who were these goofy looking

Heading out with flyers and ice-cream sandwiches in tow

54

white folks suddenly entering their domain? We certainly didn't fit the profile of drug customers. I handed him a flyer and said that we wanted to help some kids with their reading. He studied the flyer for a moment.

He looked up at me and said, "That's a good thing. Now, what's in the cooler?"

"Ice cream sandwiches," I said.

"Can we have some?"

"Sure!"

He called over the rest of the guys to grab one. Then he said, "Go ahead."

I wasn't expecting that kind of greeting when we started out. I figured we would just show up, knock on some doors and hand out ice cream to some happy children. But here we were, being cautiously welcomed by a crew of young men who offered us permission to proceed.

Since there were several buildings in the complex, our team decided to split up. As I entered the first building, I noticed that there was a young male stationed inside. He seemed to be keeping an eye on me. Maybe this was my imagination. As I made my way up the stairwell to the second and third floor apartments, I noticed what appeared to be several bullet holes in the plexiglass windows. I decided I didn't want to linger any more than I had to, so I quickened my pace a bit.

Most people were very receptive to the invitation and, of course, the ice cream. By the time we gathered back together to leave, children seemed to descend on us from everywhere. Word of the ice cream had spread. We happily gave the rest away and then made a somewhat hasty exit while attempting to appear nonchalant. After gathering back at the house, we debriefed

I managed to snap a picture on my way up the stairs.

about our experience. It was truly new territory for all of us. While we had all experienced some level of anxiety, we felt as if we had accomplished something good.

The following Wednesday, six new children, three siblings and their three cousins, showed up for the Reading Club. They lived in a two-bedroom apartment with their moms and their two dogs. Over the next few weeks, they continued to join us. One was a five-year-old boy who came along with his older brother and sister. The first couple of weeks, I literally had to pick him up in my arms and walk around with him during the reading time because he was so out of control. While doing this, he would proceed to "shoot the bird" to the other children whenever we'd walk by them. As you can imagine, this would elicit loud and colorful responses from the children who happened to be the recipient of his finger waving. Physical altercation was not out of the question. Once again, we were facing a steep learning curve.

When it was time for them to go home, I couldn't bear the thought of these young children, much less the five-year-old, having to cross the busy Midlothian Turnpike by themselves. So, I would walk them down to the corner and cross the street with them and wave goodbye as they headed up to their apartment complex. The five-year-old would ask me to carry him as we walked. Of course, his siblings and cousins would laugh and make fun of him. It was during one of these walks that I realized how much this young boy was craving love and attention. My heart began to break for him. On my solitary walks back to the house, I often wondered what their home life was like.

With the addition of these new children, it didn't take long for word of our reading club to spread among the children in the neighborhood. Over the next year, our club grew from ten to twenty to thirty children. On any given night, we had no idea who was going to show up. We had multiple teenage boys walking a mile from a local housing project. They brought all their personalities with them. This would often lead to challenging situations and conversations. Before long, we had to separate the children by age and gender to have some sense of order and effectiveness.

When the children would first arrive on a Wednesday night, it would always be a little chaotic. Initially, we tried to gather for reading time and then eat afterwards. We soon recognized that a lot of the children were hungry when they showed up, so we decided to eat first and then read. Once the mealtime was done, we read one-on-one with the younger kids while the older kids met as a group. It always amazed me when the noise and confusion would transition into the hum of children reading, reverberating throughout the house. Some nights, I felt like I was on holy ground.

Not every night was this peaceful. Some of our volunteers grew frustrated with the lack of respect some of the kids showed them. Colorful language would often emerge from some of our youngest participants. The sometimes-crude language and ill-mannered behavior inevitably led to some challenging conversations with well-intentioned adult volunteers who thought we should have better control of the children. It was challenging on the one hand because I assumed that those who came to serve would understand the challenges that these kids brought with them. On the other hand, I was dealing with my own frustration and uncertainty of how to navigate this.

The adults started staying back after the children left to regroup and discuss the evening. While one volunteer might express frustration over their experience that night, another would be overjoyed with theirs. The weekly debriefs proved to be a great source of encouragement to us all.

We came to realize a couple of important realities. One was, how can we expect a child who lives in considerable chaos at home to suddenly turn that off like flipping a switch? If their inappropriate behavior and language had been years in the making, how could we expect to change it overnight? Was it our place to even try? Don't get me wrong. There were plenty of times when I tried to do that but would often be left with more frustration. It wasn't just me. Some of the older teens would get frustrated with the younger children as well. One teenage girl once told me, "You need to yell more, Mr. Peters."

I've heard somewhere that the kids who need the most love will ask for it in the most unloving ways. Well, if that's the case, then a lot of these children needed a whole lot of love. Could we give it to them? And what would that look like?

What would emerge in the coming months, was an understanding that we would simply love these children-right where they were, in all their messiness, not treating them as some kind of improvement project. We would simply love them-unconditionally. Though I didn't realize it at the time, it was us adults who needed a little fixing of our own. As we spent more time with the children, we would find our hearts softening and our eyes opening to realities that we knew very little about.

It was during this time that we first became aware of the *Adverse Childhood Experiences* study I mentioned earlier. Gaining knowledge of childhood trauma proved tremendously helpful with our understanding of some of the children's behavior and increased our patience when they would be triggered in certain situations. For example, we had a three-year-old who was brought to the reading club by his 8-year-old uncle. He would often end up under a table with his hands over his ears, completely shut down. Initially, our approach was to tell him to get out from under the table and take a seat with the other kids. After Becky had some trauma training with a local organization called Child Savers, she would get down on the floor with him and help him relax until he was able to reason again. This was transformative in our interactions with the children going forward.

As you might imagine, it didn't take very long for us to outgrow our place. As word of the Reading Club had spread among some of our friends, a local church offered to host us. It was another transition that required us to transport the children to the church, but we were happy to have our house back. The last night we met in our house, we had forty-six children along with twelve adult volunteers.

One Wednesday evening, Becky asked the children if they had gone to church the previous Easter Sunday. Not one of them had gone. This was eye opening to us. We had assumed that many families in the African-American community were involved in local churches. After prayerfully sitting with this for a while, we decided to start having church services for them. Just like the reading club, we initially met in our home on Sunday afternoons before moving it to the same church where the reading club was now being held.

We would begin each service with several children accompanying an adult leading us in a time of singing. We had a wonderful African-American young man who would lead this time of worship for us. He sang and played guitar. The children would join him with a variety of instruments including snare drum, djembe, a shaker, and their beautiful voices.

Once, I was sitting next to one of the six-year-old boys during the service. This was the same child who Becky had sat under the table with when he was 3 years old. As we were singing the song "Break Every Chain," he leaned over to me and mumbled something. I asked him if he could repeat it.

He said, "Mr. Peters, you feel God? You feel God in our heart?"

I said, "Yes, I do. I feel God in my heart."

This was a pinch me moment. I would have many of these moments over the years. They would often serve as encouragement for me to continue amid the many challenges that we faced.

After a time of worship, we would break out into small groups for Sunday school. With little background in church, the bible and bible stories were brand new for many of the children. My class had several young boys around ten to twelve years old. One Sunday, I was sharing a story about God's love and forgiveness for us. I discussed how we can talk to God about anything we have done. He welcomes our honesty, receives us and forgives us.

Sometimes there are no words needed

After talking about it for a few minutes, I decided to put it into practice. I shared a childhood experience where I had done something I knew was wrong. When I was around 8 years old, my friends and I went on a bike ride and pulled over on the side of the street to hang out for a bit. While sitting there, one of my friends noticed a drainpipe next to the ditch near where we were sitting. He started stuffing the pipe with mud. I joined him in damming up this pipe. Who knows why we do some of the stupid things we do as kids.

Suddenly, we heard the loud voice of a man in the yard from where the pipe must have originated. We jumped on our bikes and took off as fast as we could as the man ran toward us and yelled for us to come back. The feeling of guilt was growing stronger and stronger within me. I stopped. As my friends continued their escape, I slowly turned my bike around and headed back to the scene of the crime. The man was kind and somewhat surprised that I had returned. I apologized and cleaned the mud out of the pipe under his close supervision. I left feeling better about myself, but I was probably going to get some ribbing from my friends for going back. While I had apologized to this man all those years ago, I had never talked to God about it. So, after sharing this story with the boys at the table, we bowed our heads, and I asked God for his forgiveness.

Next it was a young boy's turn to share.

Very nonchalantly he said, "One time I set the woods on fire."

Gulp! I'm not sure what I was expecting from him, but that wasn't it. He seemed comfortable sharing this with us. I think he felt safe. We turned to prayer, and he asked for forgiveness.

We went around the room with each child confessing something until it came back to me. At which time, the boy who started the fire said, "it's your turn again Mr. Peters." Well, I guess we all have a pretty long list.

Another Sunday, we had a challenging situation arise between a couple of third graders. For the sake of anonymity, let's call the rambunctious boy, Dayon and the girl, Angela. Angela had lived in a motel before recently moving in with her aunt. On this particular day, something happened between Dayon & Angela, and I saw Dayon racing for the door. I had no idea what was going on, but I sensed Dayon needed some settling down. I had him come back inside and sit in a chair for a time out while I helped set up for our meal. The meal was a special conclusion after our church service each Sunday. Dayon's restless self didn't like the ten-minute time out I had given him.

After returning him to his chair several times, he said, "Mr. Peters, can we have a talk?"

As I sat down next to him, he suddenly blurted out, "I'm sorry I called Angela homeless!"

A moment of clarity and confession emerged. I explained to him that it

60

wasn't Angela's fault that she was in this situation and that she had no control over her circumstances. I asked him if he could imagine how hard it must be for her and how sad she must feel sometimes. Suddenly, it was like heaven breaking in! He got it! I saw genuine sorrow.

He said, "I'm sorry I hurt her."

I found Angela. "Dayon has something he'd like to say to you."

She wanted no part of it. I explained to her how sorrowful he felt and what he had told me. She still wanted none of it.

About twenty minutes later, Angela called me over and said, "Mr. Peters, can you bring that boy over to talk to me now?"

I brought Dayon over to her and said, "How did that make you feel when you called Angela 'homeless'?

He said, "Good!"

Are you kidding me?!! My thought of this going sideways seemed to be fulfilling itself right in front of my eyes. Well, at least he was being honest.

I then said, "How do you feel about calling her homeless when it's not her fault?"

Dayon said, "Sad. I'm sorry!" We looked at Angela to see her response.

She said, "I ain't saying nothin!"

It was then that Angela's cousin who had come with her piped in. "She forgives you!"

No objection came from Angela. I think that was a win.

This was difficult and demanding work and was challenging for our adult volunteers who were already working with many of these children at our reading club. We needed more help. I originally thought that by having our services on Sunday afternoons at 4:00, we might attract volunteers from other churches since most churches meet on Sunday mornings. However, this did not materialize. We continued the Sunday gatherings for a couple of years, but ultimately, we had to stop meeting. The place that was currently hosting us changed hands and was no longer available to us. As we were considering our next location, the pandemic hit, and we never resumed the church services for the children.

And although we were sad that we had to stop meeting as a church, we were encouraged by a new initiative that was emerging from the Reading Club. The Neighborhood Literacy Center was about to be birthed. While we were witnessing consistency in the reading club, and the joy of reading for some of the children, we recognized that many of them needed much more help than we were able to offer. We were about to gain an even deeper understanding of the literacy gaps these children were living with. When new children would show up for Reading Club, we often noticed how far behind they seemed to be in reading. One day, a new kid showed up. He was in ninth grade at George Wythe High School. I made the mistake of having him sit with me and a younger kid to read together. My thought was that he would be an encouragement to the younger child. When his turn came, he could read the words, *the* and *a*. That was it. I became aware that I was embarrassing him. He never returned. I felt awful about this.

This jarring experience led me to some research. What I discovered was that a child living in poverty and not reading at grade level by third grade is eight times more likely to drop out of school. While I was anecdotally aware of this, I hadn't considered the magnitude. I began to compare the drop-out rates and on-time graduation rates with the literacy scores of Richmond Public Schools. What I found was shocking, at least to me. My eyes were being opened to a fundamental problem facing our communities.

From 2017-2024, The drop-out rate for RPS (Richmond Public Schools) fluctuated between 15-24%. The on-time graduation rate was between 71-79%. The chronic absenteeism rate (defined as missing 10% or more of classes) was between 16-24%.

What about the literacy rates? One of the elementary schools populated by children living in predominantly subsidized housing had a 26.7% pass-rate for third grade reading scores during the 2023-2024 school year. They were ranked 1111 out of 1114 elementary schools in Virginia. Compare this with another elementary school in a more affluent section of Richmond. That accredited school had a 90.6% reading pass-rate in third grade This school was ranked 67 out of 1114 elementary schools in Virginia.

As I shared some of what I was learning with a pastor friend of mine, he suggested the idea of starting a literacy center for the children. A place where we weren't just reading with the children, like Matthew's Place, but were teaching reading lessons to those who were falling through the cracks in the school system, those growing up in the "womb of injustice." There was a retired reading specialist who had recently come alongside us in our Reading Club. She agreed to work with me in getting the center started. The Neighborhood Literacy Center was born.

Since I had no previous experience in literacy, I attended a training seminar in a reading program called Wilson Reading System. This is a phonetical based, student paced, one-on-one curriculum. We started with two brothers. I worked with the oldest who was a second grader, and I quickly discovered that although he was half-way through the school year, he still didn't know all his letters and their sounds. Could he ever catch up?

Our first few weeks consisted of him rolling around on the floor under the table as I would show him sound cards. Being a newbie at teaching and already insecure in my ability to help him, I wasn't sure where this was headed. However, with the training we had received in trauma and with God's grace, I was able to exercise much patience and endurance. I soon came to realize that, while he wasn't in his chair for 50% of the lesson, he was listening and picking up on things. It was a happy day when we completed book one of the program.

I would pick the brothers up from school in the afternoons and drive them to our literacy center. One afternoon when I stepped into the school office, I was greeted by the school counselor. She asked me if I had a moment. Uh-Oh. I never knew what I might be told about how their school day had gone. It was not unusual for them to already be in the office for something that had happened prior to my arrival. Some days, I would find one of the boys asleep in the assistant principal's office. On this day, however, there was a smile on her face. She wanted me to know that the older boy had won the spelling bee for his class that day. Can you imagine the smile that crossed my face and the joy that welled up in my heart? I was beaming.

Over the next couple of years, we worked through the subsequent books and lessons. During his fifth-grade testing, he had successfully mastered phonics patterns and high frequency (sight) words. He still needed help with comprehension, but he now had a chance in middle school. This experience helped shape our focus for the literacy center going forward. Our goal is to see the children reading at grade level or above by time they enter middle school.

Our first students in the center came from relationships we already had with our Reading Club children and their families. However, after developing a relationship with a couple of the elementary schools, we started receiving referrals from them and having to recruit more volunteers. The need is huge. We have an incredibly faithful and flexible volunteer team, but we could easily double, triple or quadruple it. It's never an issue to find students.

I never dreamed that I would one day be the director of a literacy center. That was not on my radar at all. Even though it started with that literal dream of the young boy asking for help, it has been a gradual unfolding as I took each step, even the faltering ones.

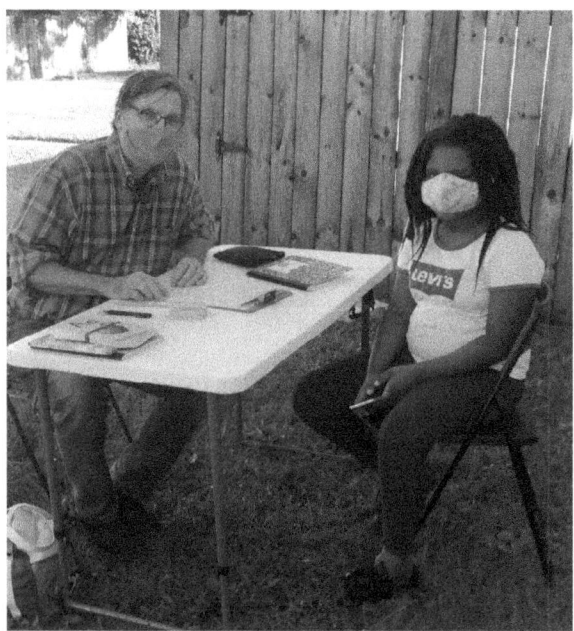

Navigating those early and uncertain days of the pandemic

I do have a dream now, though. It's to see literacy centers birthed in every community that has an elementary school nearby. With the transportation issues for many of the families, this can make it more accessible for the students and parents and allow the respective neighborhoods to be involved, perhaps as volunteers or a ministry partner. For example, at our current location, we have people from a local church who deliver healthy snacks each week for the children. I would love to come alongside a church or non-profit located near one of the schools in our city. We would initially resource them, provide training and work with them for a semester. And then, release it to them-give it away. We don't own this; we are simply stewards of the dream.

We have a real opportunity before us to bring change to the lives of these precious children. And while there are very real systemic issues that need to be addressed in our school systems, the children can't wait for these changes to occur. They need our help now-today.

Chapter 7

Hearing Their Cry

*Is not this the kind of fasting I have chosen: to loosen the chains of injustice
and untie the cords of the yoke, to set the oppressed free and break every yoke?*
Isaiah 58:6

John Woolman was a Quaker who lived during the 18th century. God moved on his heart to bring an end to all slave holdings within the Society of Friends (Quakers). He traveled throughout New England speaking at various gatherings for Quakers. At one such gathering in Philadelphia, where they were considering this issue, John sat for a lengthy period in silence and prayer.

Eventually, he stood and said, "my mind is led to consider the purity of the divine Being and the justice of His judgment, and herein my soul is covered with awfulness. Many slaves on this continent are oppressed and their cries have entered into the ears of the Most High. In infinite love and goodness he hath opened our understanding from one time to another concerning our duty towards this people, and it is not a time for delay."

John was pointing out that God had heard the cries of the enslaved and was calling his followers to join him in doing something about it. This reminds me of the story in the book of Exodus where God spoke to Moses from the burning bush. He said to Moses, "I have indeed seen the misery of my people in Egypt. I have heard them crying out because of their slave drivers, and I am concerned about their suffering." He then invited Moses to join him in bringing the people to freedom. Even with his initial reluctance, Moses went. And God was with him.

After launching the reading club on Wednesday evenings, our home suddenly became a magnet for neighborhood children looking for something to do after school. One Wednesday, we had two brothers, age three and five show up with their eight year old uncle. In the coming months, they would become regulars at the reading club.

We were heartbroken when we learned that they had been evicted from the house they were renting and were now homeless. Over the course of several weeks, they bounced from one cheap motel to another along Midlothian Turnpike in south Richmond. The entire family crammed into one motel room. Eventually, the grandmother got a job at a McDonalds within walking distance of one of the motels. This provided minimal income and allowed them to get food whenever she was working. Our church assisted them several times with food and their motel bill during this period. Eventually they found their way to a friend's apartment in a local public housing complex nearby.

By this time all three boys were in the local elementary school. Becky wanted to make sure they weren't missing school since they were now living outside their school zone. There was transportation provided by the school system, but they often missed the rides. Becky made it a point to pick them up each morning and drive them to school.

One day, I filled in for Becky. After meandering to the back of the housing project, I texted Mom to send the kids out. I waited a few minutes, hoping they would come out to the car, but no one appeared. I made my way up the stairwell to their third-floor apartment. I knocked several times, but no one answered. I was beginning to get frustrated with the mother for not having the children ready to go.

After raising the intensity of my knocking, I eventually heard a sleepy voice say, "Who is it?"

I yelled back, "It's Mr. Peters!"

The door slowly opened. There was an air mattress next to the door with six people sleeping end-to-end on it. They all appeared to be teenagers. Another child was sleeping half upright on a love seat. One of the boys I was picking up was sound asleep in an upright chair in the corner of the room; another child was asleep on the floor. *How many people are in the bedrooms?*

I finally roused the boys and watched as they searched for their shoes. They followed me out the door wearing the clothes they had slept in. Following a brief fight over who got to sit where in my car, we had a quiet ride. As we pulled up in front of the school, I said a quick prayer with them to have a good day. To which they responded with a hearty, "Amen!"

I sat there for a minute as I watched them make their way up the sidewalk and into the massive school building already teeming with life, thinking there is no way these kids could possibly be focused and stay awake in class. My heart broke for them. I felt the innocence in their spirits and their trusting nature, trusting themselves to the decisions of the adults in their lives. I can't count the times I've dropped them off somewhere then cried out to God for their protection on my way home.

Somewhere along the way it's dawned on me that God hears their cry. *How many tears have rolled down their cheeks? How many tears have been stifled because it's not cool to cry?* I know that God sees their tears and knows their fears. This does bring me some level of comfort, recognizing that they aren't left alone, that God is close.

Psalm 34:18 says, "The Lord is close to the brokenhearted and saves those who are crushed in spirit."

And yet, this raises another question for me. *Have we heard the cries of the children?* My prayer throughout the writing of this book is that I can somehow express God's heart for the children in such a way that it is experienced by you, the reader. I pray that our hearts might be open to hearing God's invitation to join Him in hearing the cries of the children as well.

What cries are being heard by God today? Is God hearing the cries of the children who have lost their fathers or mothers to violence, addiction, overdose, abandonment or incarceration?

How about an eight-year-old child who asks repeatedly if we can stop by Granny and Pop Pop's house hoping that his father might be there this time, only to find out that he's moved to North Carolina.

Does God hear his cry?

How about a young girl who's living in a seedy motel with her mom and dad as her father pimps out Mom for cash to survive. She hears the gunshots as a neighbor is murdered a couple of rooms down. Then she asks if she can bring a couple of her new friends from the motel to church. She now finds herself a mom at sixteen.

Does God hear her cry?

What about the nine-year-old child who tells you that he heard gunshots while playing at the park. He races across the street to the parking lot of his apartment only to find his stepfather lying on the asphalt, twitching as he breathes his last breaths-a finger missing and blood on the ground. He then goes into his apartment and wants to punch the flat screen TV but then decides not to.

Has God heard his cry?

What about us? Do we hear their cry?

Perhaps you're thinking, *it's all too much. I'm already overwhelmed with my own heartaches, my own family, and not to mention the world's problems constantly bombarding me through my news feed. I can't begin to enter the kind of pain you're describing. I just don't have the capacity.*

Believe me, I understand. These thoughts can bring a sense of helplessness and hopelessness. I have them, too. I can't begin to count the times I've driven away from a child's apartment or house with a rising anger in my heart and sense of despair, wishing I could do more. Will I ever be able to truly make a difference? The chasm seems too wide at times.

However, it's from this place of helplessness that I believe we are best positioned to make a difference. I believe God hears our cry as well. Our cry for meaning in life and to do something that truly matters. Our cry for peace. Our cry for hope. Our cry for a less callous heart, one that has the capacity to sit with another person's pain and be a witness to hope. How can we enter the pain of another when our emotional tank is sitting near empty?

Perhaps a better question to ask is, does God have the capacity? Does God have the emotional bandwidth? Can we trust God to lead and sustain us? The temptation is to look the other way, try not to think too much about it, resist reading or watching stories of the pain, or cast blame on someone else. However, I think for a lot of us it's that we just don't know what to do, how to help, or where to get involved.

God has heard the cries of the children as well as our cry of helplessness. It's imperative to recognize that we can't carry the weight of the world's problems, even though in this age of mass communication, we are continually asked to. We are aware of far more human suffering than any previous generation. The massive weight of the world's pain is God's job to shoulder, not ours.

And yet, God invites you and me to join him in comforting those who mourn. We may think to ourselves, *let me get myself together a bit and then I might be able to help someone else.* Would you allow me to challenge you on that thought?

When we think of drawing close to God, we often think of attending a church service or participating in some spiritual practice such as prayer, scripture reading, or perhaps fasting. We may not be aware that we also encounter God in our acts of service. *The Lord is close to the brokenhearted and saves those who are crushed in spirit.* He is present there. We are drawing close to God when we come near the brokenhearted.

This reality was impressed upon me one day while I was performing an x-ray exam in a local public housing project in Richmond. I pulled the portable x-ray machine into the apartment and began to make my way upstairs to the patient's bedroom. As I pulled the machine up the stairs, I noticed metal strips on each step along with the cinderblock walls to the side. It had an institutional feel to it rather than a home. I entered the bedroom and was greeted by an elderly woman lying in a hospital bed. Although she was obviously in some type of respiratory distress, a smile emerged, and she expressed her heartfelt thanks for me coming to help her.

I noticed a couple of crinkled certificates taped to the wall above her bed that honored her faithful Sunday school attendance at her church. After completing the exam, she thanked me repeatedly for my help as I was exiting her room. As I made my way down the steps, out of the apartment and back to my van, my heart broke for her. I was overcome with a sense of compassion, thinking about her genuine childlike faith and having to live in such a dark and depressive environment while being very sick on top of it.

She seemed so helpless. I spoke aloud, "Oh God, she needs so much help! What can I do? How can I help her?"

Then, I heard a reply. It wasn't audible, but it was as clear as anything I've ever heard. *You need her more than she needs you. She has more faith than you do-because she's had to.*

In that moment, I had a glimpse into the heart of God and the way he sees things so differently than I often do. I felt a sense of clarity and conviction. I had a clarity that God was with this woman in her suffering in a very tangible way. In hindsight, I had experienced God's presence through her gracious smile and greeting that she had just shared with me. It reminds me of a quote attributed to Mother Teresa who worked with the poor in Calcutta, India. She said, "If we recognize Jesus under the appearance of bread (referring to the Eucharist), we will have no difficulty recognizing him in the disguise of the suffering poor." She would go on to say, "I have an opportunity to be with Jesus 24 hours a day." She was acknowledging what Jesus had said in the Gospel of Matthew, chapter 25. Whenever we care for someone who is hungry, thirsty, a stranger, the poor, the sick or incarcerated, we are actually caring for him.

I also felt a conviction that maybe my view of ministry to the poor needed a deeper understanding. Perhaps I am the poor one, not in some financial way, but in my relationship with God. I have a shared humanity with this woman; I was most definitely on the receiving end that day.

I believe God is inviting me and you, in our own weakness and brokenness, to join him on his mission of being close to the brokenhearted in this world.

One recent morning, this truth was brought home to me again. I read a story from the bible where Jesus and his disciples had crossed the Sea of Galilee. During the journey, a storm suddenly came upon them. The disciples were terrified as they witnessed the fury of the wind and waves that was about to capsize them. Their situation seemed hopeless. What could they do? They went to get Jesus who appeared to be peacefully sleeping during all the chaos. They woke him and said, "Teacher, do you not care that we are perishing?" Jesus got up and spoke to the storm and it stopped. As you can imagine, the disciples were stunned. Who was this man who could calm a storm by simply saying, "Peace. Be still."

Well, Jesus wasn't done. His disciples were about to encounter a little more amazement. Once they had safely reached shore, they were met by a seemingly deranged man.

"As Jesus stepped ashore, a certain man from the town met him who was possessed by demons. For a long time, this man had worn no clothes and had not lived in a house, but among the tombs." Luke 8:26,27.

The story goes on to say that people had bound him in chains trying to control him, but he would break free. After a brief conversation with this man, in a similar way in which he had spoken to the storm, Jesus spoke to the demons who were possessing and tormenting this man and told them to leave. And they did. The people who witnessed this ran off to tell others, who soon came running back to see this incredible miracle.

"...they found the man from whom the demons had gone out, sitting at Jesus' feet, clothed and in his right mind, and they were afraid." Luke 8: 35

I began to try and imagine what it was like to have been present there with Jesus and this man. It was that one word, clothed, that caught my attention. Where did the clothes come from? Who clothed him? I then imagined Jesus taking off his outer garment and putting it on this man, clothing him with dignity, covering his shame. I was catching a glimpse of the kindness of God and our shared humanity. I saw this man sitting there with Jesus, free from the years of torment, perhaps laughing and enjoying the company of others for the first time in a long while. I pictured a fire cooking the fish they had just caught.

As I stood at a distance watching this beautiful, redemptive scene, I saw Jesus look up from the fire and turn his head towards me. He raised his arm, smiled, and waved for me to come and join them. Even as I sit writing this, tears are rolling down my cheek. I'm invited, I'm wanted, and I'm important to Jesus and to his mission to draw near the brokenhearted. He's heard my cry **and** the cries of the vulnerable, the marginalized, and the children living with untold heartbreak.

You're invited, you're wanted, and you're important to Jesus and his mission to comfort those who mourn.

I believe this is an invitation to each of us. In the Christian church, there are often two invitations we encounter. The first is the invitation to come to faith in Jesus for the forgiveness of our sins, recognizing that Jesus is the bridge between

God and us. This is often accompanied by the sacraments of baptism and the eucharist (communion).

The second invitation flows naturally from the first. As we step into life with God, basking in His love and acceptance of us, we begin to see others through this same paradigm of love and acceptance. This often leads us to follow Jesus into some mission opportunity. It could be answering a call to help alleviate suffering in some foreign country. Or it could be something more local, like volunteering at a food pantry, helping a child learn to read, or any place where the vulnerable need someone to come alongside them. It's no different than Jesus' disciples following him across the lake and joining him as he set this man free. While everyone saw a hopelessly damaged and deranged individual, Jesus heard his cry and set him free.

Putting our trust in Jesus and acts of service to the marginalized are both valid expressions of our faith. However, they aren't meant to be separated.

"For it is by grace you have been saved, through faith—and this is not from yourselves, it is the gift of God—not by works, so that no one can boast. For we are God's handiwork, created in Christ Jesus to do good works, which God prepared in advance for us to do." Ephesians 2:8-10

The Greek word for handiwork is *poiema*, from which our English word *poem* is derived. We are each uniquely created and gifted by God to bring beauty and healing, his kingdom into this world. We're asking for this each time we pray The Lord's Prayer, "may your kingdom come, your will be done, on earth as it is in heaven." Collectively, with God's help, we can bring our uniquely created selves to bear in a world crying out for hope. We can make a difference. And in the process, we find our own cries answered.

There are many unsung heroes presently at work, challenging the systemic issues affecting the womb of injustice I spoke of earlier, including fair housing and transportation, equitable education, and criminal justice reform to name just a few. I am very encouraged by dedicated and capable individuals I have met over the years who are doing just that. It can be a long, slow and arduous process, but it has the potential to positively affect generations to come. For me, my focus is working with the children who are currently in this womb of injustice and who can't wait until the systemic changes occur. They need our help now. We join

John Woolman and the Spirit of God who led him to speak the words, "It is not a time for delay."

Where might God be inviting you to join him? I can't answer that specifically, but God can. There's a quote by minister and theologian Frederick Buechner that I believe captures this well.

"The Place God calls you to is the place where your deep gladness and the world's deep hunger meet."

What I can answer with confidence is that God is inviting you and me to open our hearts to his invitations. His invitation to see children as He sees them and to be willing to hear their cries as He hears them. To see people of a different race as He sees them-made in His image and with infinite value, bringing beauty into this world. To see ourselves as God sees us-with a gaze of love and great joy and purpose.

That's what love does. God will meet us there and illuminate the steps that follow. We don't need to see the entire path. He will be a "lamp unto our feet" with each step we take. As we draw near, with our own imperfect lives, into the lives of others who are also brokenhearted, we will both begin to hear the voice of the one who calmed that sea. *Peace. Be still.*

CROSSING THE WATER JAMES

Questions to Ponder

Chapter One- The Formative Years

1. What were your formative years like? In what ways were you segregated from other races?

What falsehoods were you told or were formed in you more subtly?

2. Did you have a childhood friend from a different race? How did this friendship different from friendships of your own race?

3. In what ways has your upbringing shaped your worldview as it relates to the struggle of the black community?

Chapter Two- Can You Spell Naivety?

1. Have you ever intentionally entered a relationship with someone of a different race?

What was your experience like? What were some of the challenges you encountered?

2. Can you remember a time in your life when you had some racial naivety exposed?

3. What's a stereotype of another race that comes to mind? Are you willing to have it challenged?

Chapter Three- We're Ballin' Now

1. Do you have a friend of a different race today? What does your time together look like?

What do you really know about them?

2. What is one step you can take toward getting to know this person better?

3. Have you experienced a time when your heart was exposed and vulnerable? How did it make you feel? What was the outcome? Did you move toward or away from it?

Chapter Four- The Plank Eye

1. Has there ever been a time when you experienced prejudice directed towards you? How did it make you feel?

2. What are some practical ways we can be sensitive to people of a different race?

3. When have you listened to a person of another race simply with the intention to understand?

4. What questions could you ask to help facilitate understanding?

Chapter Five- The Womb of Injustice

1. What is gentrification? In what ways might this affect the poor?

2. Do you currently know someone who is living in the "womb of injustice?" What are they facing? What might be helpful to them?

3. In your opinion, what are some systemic issues that might be hindering the black community?

4. In what ways might we judge a person of another race? How can we see them through God's heart?

Chapter Six- Living the Dream

1. Have you ever had a dream, literal or otherwise, inviting you to make a difference in someone's life? Did you move toward it? What challenges did you face? What joys emerged?

2. Would the children described in this chapter be welcome in your church? Your home? What might some of the challenges be?

3. How would you imagine Jesus interacting with these children?

Chapter Seven- Hearing Their Cry

1. Read the Book of Isaiah, chapter 58. What is the contrast being pointed out?

Why do you think this passage begins with the exhortation to, "Shout it aloud, do not hold back?"

2. What cries might be reaching the ears of God, today?

3. What cries have you heard?

4. What might be a first step in moving toward the cry you are hearing?

5. When contemplating this, what fears/anxieties arise? Consider asking God for the *grace of courage* to take that first step.

Acknowledgments

God, you've given me just a glimpse into your heart for humanity. I join you in desiring to see the world to catch it as well.

Becky, this journey is ours together. Thank you for our life of adventure and giving me permission to share it as I experienced it- except when I had some details wrong. I appreciate your clearsighted view of things, but most of all-your heart.

My children, thank you for taking this journey with us. While I'm acutely aware that you had no choice in the matter and there were many, many challenges along the way, my deep hope is that your lives have been enriched because of it. And thank you for your honest feedback on the manuscript and initiating some good conversation about your experiences growing up in South Richmond.

Richard Verlander, I am grateful for you giving me a kick in the rear to move this project forward. Sincerely, thank you for your genuine encouragement and support. I felt you alongside me throughout the process.

Wayne Dementi, thank you for your publishing experience, wisdom and enthusiasm. I always leave our conversations encouraged and more confident.

Kathryn Starke, you've helped me come to appreciate red ink-well, I'm trying. Thank you for not letting up or letting me off the hook. Your publishing and literacy experience has proven invaluable in bringing this work to fruition.

Jayne, your quiet, behind the scenes work is noticed and appreciated.

Don Coleman, thank you for being a friend through the years, a sounding board through this process and encouraging me when I was struggling with doubt. I feel your prayers.

Peggy, Dan, Jim and Vickie, your prayers throughout this project were a source of great encouragement-and a very real help.

Ann, the literacy center has carried your heart from the beginning. Thank you for your clear- eyed, no-nonsense approach from day one. You always showed up with your big ol' heart. Your willingness to read to a sleeping child blesses me to this day. Thank you!

Barbara and MiMi, you were faithful to your last breath. I am humbled. Great is your reward in heaven.

To everyone who has come alongside our work with the children, some who are no longer with us, we did this together-Thank you! There is fruit that remains.

Lastly, to all the children who have crossed my path these past few years, I am the richer one for it.

About the Author

Ken was born in Richmond, Virginia and received a BS degree in Radiology Administration from Virginia Commonwealth University in 1983. He worked in the radiology field for several years prior to answering a call to ministry. He spent a year at Asbury Seminary in Wilmore, Kentucky before returning to Richmond to help plant a church. Ken and his wife, Becky planted the Richmond Vineyard (The Bridge RVA) church in 1995 which they've pastored for nearly 30 years. In 2019, the church launched The Neighborhood Literacy Center where he and a faithful team of volunteers work with children from Richmond Public Schools, helping them achieve grade-level reading prior to entering middle-school.

www.ingramcontent.com/pod-product-compliance
Lightning Source LLC
Chambersburg PA
CBHW051228120626
46547CB00013B/1551